10/8/15
$40.95

Gonzague Masquelier

GESTALT THERAPY:
Living Creatively Today

from *VOULOIR SA VIE, la Gestalt-thérapie aujourd'hui*

éditions RETZ, Paris, 1999

translation by Sally Reeder Cojean

A GestaltPress Book

**published and distributed by
Routledge
Taylor & Francis Group**

Copyright 2006 by   The GestaltPress
127 Abby Court
Santa Cruz, CA 95062

and   165 Route 6A
Orleans, MA 02653

email gestaltpress@aol.com, gestaltpress@comcast.net

Distributed by   Routledge, Taylor and Francis Group
711 Third Avenue, New York, NY 10017, USA
2 Park Square, Milton Park, Abingdon, Oxon OX14 4RN

Library of Congress Cataloging-in-Publishing Data

ISBN: 0-88163-458-1

To my four children:
Timothée, Célestine, Barnabé and Corentin

GONZAGUE MASQUELIER
5 rue du Pressoir Coquet
60 000 BEAUVAIS
FRANCE

gonzague.masquelier@wanadoo.fr

December 2002

SUMMARY

PART TWO

A THERAPY OF THE HERE AND NOW

PART THREE

CONTEMPORARY GESTALT

Introduction:
Understanding Gestalt Therapy

G estalt comes from the German verb *gestalten* which means "to give form or structure to." Gestalt Therapy is particularly involved with "contact": how do we make contact with ourselves, with others, with our environment? Gestalt psychotherapy specializes in what we call the "contact-boundary," that is to say, the place where information, desires and material needs meet. This boundary is moving all the time, it is our way of being in the world, of having relationships.

Many therapeutic approaches try to explain our psyche in terms of entities (the Id, the Ego and the Super Ego in psychoanalysis), or in observational grids (as in the three states of Ego in transactional analysis—parent, adult and child) or in body blockages (bioenergetics), etc.

Gestalt Therapy takes us from the age of photography to the age of cinema. That is, it is concerned with "the process," the constant adjustment between an organism and its environment. This adjustment is in a state of constant change. As a result, contact is never static, in the way a photograph captures an expression or a gesture. Gestalt Therapy speaks of the contact cycle, of creative adjustment, of form which emerges from content —these are all expressions which evoke movement, the cinema and the theatre. "Living creatively," in the title of this book, means growing and continually inventing new ways of being in the world.

A humanistic approach

Gestalt Therapy is therefore both a science, with rigorous analytical tools, and an art of living, since it contributes to making life more harmonious and varied. It is, above all, a psychotherapeutic approach, that is, an approach which allows, within a given structure, the exploration of existential difficulties.

Its originality does not, therefore, lie in its techniques which we shall evoke in the second part, but rather in its objectives: to open up the field of our potential, to increase our ability to adapt to different people and environments, to restore our freedom of choice.

Gestalt Therapy is rightfully included in the movement of humanistic psychotherapies. In ancient Greece the *therapeutris* was a servant of the temple, given the task of taking care of the statues of the gods; looking after them, decorating them, honoring them.[1] I like the etymology of the word: the therapist is therefore not "a doctor," who supposedly knows everything and therefore has the power to heal the neurosis of the patient, but rather a person who puts him or herself at the service of a human being in difficulty, to help that person regain or preserve dignity and beauty.

The prefix "psycho" also comes from the Greek: *psuckhé*, which means breath, the vital energy, the seat of the emotions. It also means butterfly, symbol of the immortality of the soul.[2] The psychotherapist is therefore the one who helps a person to maintain or regain his vital breath.

---

[1] Ginger S.and A., *La Gestalt, une thérapie de contact,* Paris, Hommes et Groupes, 1995
(first edition 1987)

[2] As for *Psyche*, she was the most exceptionally beautiful princess, with whom Cupid, God of love, fell in love...

This therapeutic movement, which developed initially in the United States in the fifties, has been described as humanistic. The idea was to propose a third way, between psychoanalysis, which is seen as deterministic (what happened to me in my childhood conditions my existence) and behaviorism, where a given stimulus will provoke a predictable response (one must therefore change the behavior or the environment to obtain the desired answer).

Putting the relationship at the center

Gestalt is a therapy in which the client[3] is the agent of change, and the relationship is the engine of change. What happens between client and therapist is the indicator of how the person develops and maintains relationships in his or her daily life.

Therapy is therefore primarily a **place of welcome**, where human beings (professionals and clients) who have chosen this approach for its intellectual openness, for its understanding of humans in their combined physical, emotional, intellectual, social and spiritual contexts, can meet.

The "cost" of this choice, of this theoretical position, is the difficulty of describing the approach, because the richness of living relationships cannot be reduced to diagrams or techniques. Gestalt Therapy doesn't hide behind a method or analytical grid; it works with what one is, what one loves, with what is discovered along each individual's way, with the heart, but also, sometimes, with times of shadow, and fatigue.

---

[3] Gestalt psychotherapists happily use the word "client" to emphasise the active implication, while other professionals use the term "patient" with reference to the medical model.

My aims

This book is aimed at a wide public, those who are interested in psychotherapeutic trends. I have, therefore, chosen clinical examples to illustrate the different concepts rather than developing their theoretical bases, at the risk of disappointing some professionals.

A return to the origins of the Gestalt approach will introduce us to the founders. Part two will explain the principal concepts and their philosophical sources. Finally we will finish with the different fields of application and their current development in France.

ONE

THE HISTORY OF GESTALT THERAPY

Fritz and Laura Perls

F riedrich Perls, later known as Fritz, was born into a wealthy family in Berlin on July 8, 1893. He spent his childhood in the Jewish ghetto of the Berlin suburbs and was given a very typical education: he describes himself as a rebellious child from the start.[4] He soon realized the difficulty of being accepted into any form of society: his education was too liberal for the orthodox Jewish ghetto and yet as a Jew he was rejected by bourgeois German society. In 1898, his family moved to a fashionable area in the center of Berlin, but difficulties with their neighbors continued.

His father, Nathan, was in the wine trade and traveled a lot for his work; Fritz described him as a great seducer, who loved society and tried to become assimilated into German culture. He belonged to a Jewish cultural organization and was also a freemason.

His mother, Amelia, came from an orthodox Jewish family; she never finished her formal education, but loved theatre and the opera.

His parents quarreled a lot. Fritz witnessed violent arguments between them during which Nathan beat Amelia, who took her revenge by violently pulling his long beard. Fritz came to hate his father, and developed a spirit of rebellion which was never to leave him. However, he was very close to Grete, one of his two sisters.

---

[4] Shepard M., *Le Père de la Gestalt, dans l'intimité de Fritz Perls,* Montreal, Stanke, 1980.

When he was about ten years old, Fritz ran away from home for a few days, was expelled from school and committed some petty crimes. Then he discovered the theatre, was hired to be an extra and worked with the producer Max Reinhardt. This teacher insisted on the importance of emotion, on the right tone of voice and the right gesture in order to "ring true." He directed actors in a totally new way to be more themselves. Fritz was stunningly successful in the role of Mephistopheles in Goethe's *Faust*.[5]

This passion for the theatre allowed Fritz to regain, if not the esteem of his father, at least the understanding support of his mother. After an education which he described as mediocre, he began to study medicine, then psychiatry, while remaining passionate about theatre and sharing his mother's love of opera.

> *This passion for theatre production and the authentic expression of emotions would later influence his profession as a psychotherapist.*

Fritz as a soldier

The First World War interrupted his studies: in 1915 Fritz volunteered for the Red Cross and found himself in Belgium as a nurse in a unit specializing in gas attacks. He was often used as a translator because he spoke French well.

Fritz was horrified by the appalling madness of the conflict. He did not think of himself as a Jew since he was not religious. But he was sent on dangerous missions by his superior officer who explained with contempt that perhaps there would be one less Jew after the war. He sometimes wondered who his real enemies were: the British on the other side or the Germans in his own trenches. He was wounded by a shell and then suffered from lung lesions after a gas attack. He became an officer in 1917.

---

[5] All his life he would say that this role of the devil "illuminated the dark years."

He survived these trials but was profoundly shaken by his war experiences. Three defining characteristics of temperament seemed to arise from this time1: a profound humanism (for example, he protested when forbidden to nurse wounded British soldiers); a surprising ability to make quick intuitive judgments about people; and frequent feelings of disillusionment about human beings (whom he discovered to be capable of the worst atrocities).

His therapeutic journey

After the war, Fritz took up his studies again, became a neuropsychiatrist, and was a part of the artistic and rebellious circles in Berlin. He wasn't interested in psychiatry, which was seen at the time as a new but very controversial approach.

In 1926, he started therapy with Karen Horney, a dissident pupil of Freud's.[6]

This psychoanalyst emphasized the importance of the socio-cultural environment in any treatment. While putting aside the detailed exploration of the past, she emphasized present difficulties, that she saw as responsible for behavioral difficulties. She later emigrated to the United States where her ideas were taken up by the dele-first American feminist movement. She suggested that certain neuroses associated with women are brought on by the place given to women in society. Horney always stayed in contact with Perls, supported him in his research and helped him to settle in New York.

In 1927, Perls left Berlin for Frankfurt, where he took care of wounded soldiers suffering from brain damage, under the direction of Kurt Goldstein. At this time, Goldstein was

---

[6] Karen Horney (1885-1952) opposed Freud on the theme of sexuality by disagreeing with his emphasis on penis envy in women. She emphasized a basic existential *anxiety* (see chapter 5).

conducting research in *Gestalt psychology* which involved studies of how we perceive forms and how our brains produce images. There was no psychotherapeutic project in *Gestalt psychology*, and Perls later borrowed the word *Gestalt* for his therapeutic approach.

He socialized with philosophers like Buber[7] and Tillich[8] and resumed his own psychoanalysis with Clara Happel. He was interested in Bauhaus,[9] an artistic teaching organization and contemporary art movement which proposed a new teaching method: that personal experimentation by the student is more powerful than the knowledge presented externally by a professor.

His psychoanalytical journey led him to question all the imperatives which had marked his life: you must be respectable, you must earn money, you must please. Little by little he was letting these suffocating constraints go, yet he felt lost and anguished in abandoning them.

> *Here we find two themes which will be important to him in the elaboration of Gestalt Therapy: the search for authenticity and the value of experimentation (by the client with the reassuring accompaniment of the therapist).*

It was in 1928 in Frankfurt that he met his future partner…

---

[7] Martin Buber (1878-1965) was an Israeli philosopher, principally known for his writings on the dialogue relationship (I-Thou).

[8] Paul Tillich (1886-1965) was a German theologian discharged by the Nazis. Perls caught up with him again later, during conferences in Esalen.

[9] This movement was started in 1919 by W. Gropius.

The beautiful student

Lore Posner was much younger than Fritz. She was the eldest in a family of three children. She was given both the expected classical training for a young bourgeois girl of her time (needlework, piano and poetry) and a more modern education. Her father, a wealthy jeweller (change order) valued her curiosity and original intelligence and pushed her to pursue her course of studies. She therefore gave up the idea of a career as a piano soloist to study law and then psychology.

When she met Fritz, Lore found a resolution of the two polarities which were important to her: on the one hand, a need for security which was possibly fulfilled by the twelve-year age gap between them, and by Fritz's social status as a doctor and decorated war veteran; and the other pole, her need for adventure, nourished by the bohemian aspirations of this man she wanted to marry. She shared his taste for research (since she was a graduate student of *Gestalt psychology*) and his passion for art (she was already an excellent pianist and a great fan of opera).

Lore's father and brother opposed the match, and they conducted an investigation of Fritz' past and concluded that it would be a disastrous marriage. But there was nothing they could do about it. Against the wishes of her family Lore moved in with Fritz on her twentieth birthday (in 1925). Resigned, Lore's father wrote: "If I were to do anything at all against him, I would lose my daughter. And that is something that I really don't want to happen."[10]

She anglicized her name to Laura and like Fritz, began psycho-analysis with Clara Happel which originally was motivated by her

---

[10] Shepard M., *op cit.*

desire to understand her partner and his friends' jargon: "All I wanted was to be a member of the club!"[11]

Vienna, then Berlin

In 1927, Perls thought about becoming a psychoanalyst himself and left for a further year's training in Vienna with Helen Deutsch. He was disappointed by her professional coldness.

He returned to Berlin and started as a psychoanalyst in 1928.[12] Meanwhile he continued his own therapy with Eugen Harnick, which involved five sessions a week. After four years of living together, Laura asked him to marry her. Fritz wanted to work on this decision in therapy, but his analyst told him "You are not allowed to make any important decisions while you are in therapy. If you get married, I shall stop being your therapist." In his own words Perls then exchanged "psychoanalysis for marriage"[13] and married Laura in August, 1929. Their daughter Renate was born two years later. Fritz continued therapy with Wilhelm Reich, who helped him discover the potential in bodily and emotional approaches. He felt stimulated and validated by these approaches and would always say that of his four successive psychoanalysts, Reich was the most important.

The rise of Nazism interrupted this period. Reich was attacked for his Marxist positions and fled to Norway. Apart from his Jewish background, Fritz was politically left-wing, a member of the antifascist League and he gave lessons at the Worker's University: all reasons for him to be a target of the Nazis. He left hurriedly for Holland in April 1933, with a hundred marks hidden

---

[11] Perls L., *Vivre à la frontière*, Montreal, Editions du Reflet, 1993.

[12] In 1928.

[13] Perls F., *Ma Gestalt-therapie, une poubelle vue du dedans et du dehors*, Paris, Tchou, 1976.

in a cigarette lighter.[14] Laura took refuge with their two year-old baby at her parents' home in the south of Germany. In May 1933, the Nazis burned the works of Freud, Einstein, Thomas Mann and Zweig in front of the university of Berlin.

Laura joined Fritz six months later. They were not allowed to work in Holland, and so began a time of economic hardship for them. In 1934 they decided to leave for South Africa; they were attracted by the research of Prime Minister Smuts (a cofounder of the League of Nations—1919),[15] and by his global view of man and society, what he called the holistic approach.

Johannesburg

Fritz spent the three weeks of the boat trip to Johannesburg learning English intensively. The couple was attracted by the wealth and quality of life which they found in South Africa. In 1935, Fritz and Laura founded *The South African Institute of Psychoanalysis* and success came very quickly for them. They both worked full-time and built a luxurious and original house and soon their second child, Stephen, was born. Fritz became passionate about aviation and led the life of a wealthy man, with a private pool and an ice rink.

---

[14] Perls F., *op cit.*

[15] He would be involved, in 1945, in the creation of the United Nations.

In 1936, he returned to Europe, by boat—having thought of flying his own plane there[16]—to give a talk on "oral resistances" during a psychoanalytical congress in Marienbad.

Perls was very hurt by the cool reception he re-ceived when he went to visit Freud—who asked him to leave after only a few minutes! Since he felt generally constrained by orthodox psycho-analysis; both the geographical distance and the different culture in South Africa helped him to detach himself from what he called "the rigidity of analytical taboos."

Ego, Hunger and Aggression

He finished his first book, *Ego, Hunger and Aggression,* in 1940. The subtitle of the first edition was *a revision of Freud's theory and method*, and it demonstrates how much Perls had changed.[17] In this work, he disagreed with psychoanalytical theory on four principal points:

• **The place of sexuality** in the psyche was exaggerated. The author reproached analysts with never taking off their "libidinal spectacles."[18] He affirmed that the need for individual survival, demonstrated by the cries of a hungry baby, our need for security or to be recognized) was as important as the need for survival of the species (reproduction) and sexuality.

• Perls gave value to what he called **healthy aggressiveness**. To feed ourselves, we need to destroy food in order to digest it.

---

[16] He said in *In and Out the Garbage Pail,* that he had dreamed of being the first. "flying analyst" but that at the last minute, someone beat him to the second hand plane that he wanted to buy for the trip.

[17] Perls F., *Ego, Hunger and Aggression,* Durban, South Africa, 1942.
French translation, *Le Moi, la Faim et L'Agressivité,* Paris, Tchou, 1978, 334 pages.

[18] Perls F., *A life chronology,* available on the web: www.gestalt.org

The hunger instinct (for food but also for affection, for knowledge, etc.) is indispensable to our growth.[19]

• He insisted in taking **time** into account: as we can't describe a fruit without taking duration into account; it is ripe today but could be rotten next week. The author reproached Freud with presenting our repressed memories as fixed, like "sardines in a tin," and affirmed that there was no other reality than the present.

• Finally, Perls reproached psychoanalysis with not giving enough importance to **body work**. At the end of the book he described relaxation exercises, visualization exercises, to diversify work on resistance: there is a thread running through this part of the book of what would become future gestalt intervention strategies. The author proposed the term "concentration therapy" in opposition to "association therapy."

He entrusted the manuscript to Marie Bonaparte, a friend and disciple of Freud's, during an encounter at the Cape. She responded, "If you don't believe in the theory of the libido, you ought to resign from psychoanalysis..." Perls, shocked by this declaration which he described as anti-scientific,[20] because it was put forward as a belief system, retorted, "Is libido theory an act of faith?" That was an important moment in the divergence between Perls and psychoanalysis. He did not resign, but his relationship with the Institute of Psychoanalysis diminished little by little.

> *It seems important to me to know the lives of the great pioneers of therapy so as to arrive at a better understanding of what they bring that is new. One cannot build a theory or a psychological approach "ex nihilo." Each person rests first on what he has lived, on his experience, on his vision of the world.*

---

[19] We will take up this theme in chapter six, regarding the gestalt intervention.

[20] Perls F., *A life chronology op. cit.*

> *Freud, who has been described as having a phobia about looking people in the eye and being ill at ease in contact with people, constructed for psychoanalytical treatment, an extremely distanced framework, by sitting behind the patient who was lying down on a sofa. Perls, who was an agitator and liked contact with people, preferred a more confrontational formula.*
>
> *Freud, who was an archeology enthusiast, who collected Egyptian statues, directed himself toward shedding light on the past. Perls abandoned everything to start from scratch a dozen times in his life: one can easily understand how his focus on the "here and now—what am I deciding to do?" was a precious aid to him.*

In 1942, he volunteered for the army on the British side: he served as a doctor and an officer. Having taken part in two successive world wars, but on opposing sides, Perls was disillusioned and cynical about political ideas,[21] and the big ideas which artificially unite a nation. This brought out in him an attention to and great compassion for individual suffering. He was a gruff anarchist, with a big heart.

At the end of the war, in 1946, the Perlses were worried by the rise of fascism in South Africa and decided to move to the United States. Fritz left first to prepare the way for Laura and the two children, who would join him later.[22]

---

[21] Personal notes taken during a conference address by Stephen Perls in Montreal in 1993; this text is available on the web at www.gestalt.org under the title: *A son's reflections.*

[22] Renate was then fifteen and Stephen eleven.

Fritz PERLS

The American years

At the age of fifty-three and with the help of friends who were psychoanalysts, including Karen Horney, Fritz rapidly built up a practice in New York. His book, *Ego, Hunger and Aggression,* was republished in London (1947) and his innovative approach developed as he abandoned the couch and began his first groups. After fifteen months of separation, he was reunited with Laura and the children.[23]

Paul Goodman, a writer and man of the theatre, introduced him into artistic and anti-establishment circles in New York. Fritz spent time with Merce Cunningham, who was developing contemporary dance, and with Julian and Judith Beck, the creators of Living Theatre, with whom he rediscovered his passion for the stage. All these artists were sexually "liberated" and socially provocative.

Fritz suffered more and more from the disassociation between his image as a respectable therapist and his personal life, which was becoming more and more unrestrained, especially sexually. However, what was permissible for jazz musicians and actors was not so acceptable for a psychotherapist. His provocations therefore distanced him from the more traditional professionals and thus, Paul Goodman's friendship became all the more precious to him.

---

[23] Autumn 1947.

Goodman

Who was this man who was to have such a profound influence on the development of Gestalt Therapy? He was a typical urbanite, born in Greenwich Village, in the heart of New York, in 1911. When he was very young, his father deserted the family and his mother took on odd jobs for the survival of her family. Paul was principally brought up by his sister Alice, who was ten years or so older than him. After an easy passage through school, he went on to earn a university literary degree. He was passionate about philosophy, anthropology and art history.

Paul GOODMAN

Paul knew of Fritz from his first book, and was probably the first New York intellectual to discover Reich. In 1946, he began psychotherapy under Lowen, a student of Reich's and the future founder of bio-energetics.

Goodman and the Perls all had solid psychoanalytical backgrounds but felt constrained by the Freudian doctrine. Art was also a link between them: Fritz and the theatre, Laura and music, Paul and literature.

© G.Masquelier

The group of seven

A work and training group,[24] the "group of seven" met every week in the Perls' apartment and little by little new concepts were defined, in particular thanks to Goodman, who gave form to Fritz's intuitions. Laura would declare, years later: "It was essentially to him that we owed the elaboration of a coherent theory of Gestalt psychotherapy."[25]

Other members of this work group marked the origins of Gestalt, in particular Paul Weisz, who was passionate about Zen. He brought his knowledge of eastern philosophy to the group and suggested that they concentrate on the *here and now*, emphasizing the importance of not separating the head from the body in psychotherapeutic work. "You were one of the rare people that I listened to in my life," Fritz wrote to him.[26]

Isadore From, through his great philosophical erudition, encouraged the group to refine the theoretical conceptualization of Gestalt, but he wasn't a writer.

Eliott Shapiro ran a "progressive" school based on active teaching methods for disturbed children.[27] He helped the group to put a form to experiments concerning their research. This approach, this desire for *learning by doing*, can be found throughout the development of Gestalt Therapy.

Let us not forget that of the seven people who made up the crucible of Gestalt, five were long-settled Americans, anchored in their original culture. This meeting between the Perls' European culture (including their passion for philosophy and phenome-

---

[24] Fritz and Laura Perls, Paul Goodman, Paul Weisz, Elliot Shapiro, Isadore From, Sylvester Eastman.

[25] Perls L., *Vivre à la frontière, op.cit.*

[26] Perls F., *Ma Gestalt-thérapie, une poubelle vu du dedans et du dehors, op. cit.*

[27] A pedagogical approach which would become famous with A. S. Neill's British experiment and his book, *Summerhill.*

nology) and the pragmatism (desire for efficiency and empiricism) of their American counterparts gave birth to a movement which would respect both these tendencies.

Finding a name

The discussions around the choice of a name for this new vision of man were lively and allow us a glimpse of what each brought to the construction of the building. Fritz first thought of "concentration therapy," which he evoked in his first book; he wanted to emphasize the idea of a conscious awareness of the body and of feelings, which one gets by concentrating on the here and now. Laura preferred the term "existential therapy," but this seemed too linked to Sartre, who was not well-accepted in the United States during the Macarthy era. Hefferline suggested "integrative therapy."

Fritz then suggested "Gestalt Therapy," with reference to the work on Gestalt theory, that Laura in particular had studied for her doctorate on visual perception. Laura and Goodman rejected the idea at first, finding their work to be far from the concepts of Gestalt theory, and worried that it might be too esoteric. Little by little, the work group finally all agreed on the name.

Then several Gestalt theoreticians who had emigrated to the United States expressed their reservations, as did Lewin who thought that they were "appropriating" the word *Gestalt*. It was Goodman who took on the responsibility of addressing the controversy, some years later, as he said ironically: "It's probable that if the expression *Gestalt* had not been chosen in 1951 and had remained associated only with the perception of forms, it would now be gathering dust in the stacks of university libraries!"[28]

Gestalt Therapy

Fritz brought back a hundred or so pages of notes from South Africa on what might be a new therapeutic approach. He offered Goodman five hundred dollars to help him put these thoughts into better shape and to complete them. Fritz was brilliant in his clinical inspirations and his theoretical intuitions but he was not a talented writer, especially in English, which was not his mother tongue.

Paul was a poet and man of letters but he was much more than just the ghost writer Fritz was looking for at first, and introduced many original concepts in his expanding of the material. A third writer joined them, Hefferline, who was a university professor and who tested a certain number of experiments on his students and then wrote detailed papers on them.

Two volumes emerged from the collective writing of Perls, Goodman and Hefferline. In 1951, the publisher first brought out a collection of experiments, to which Hefferline made a major contribution, because the American tendency at this time was to give value to such practical subjects.[29] This commercial choice turned out to be a mistake, since it diverted the reading public away from the professionals to whom these writings were originally addressed.

The collaboration between Fritz and Paul for the theoretical volume, to be published next, was not easy. The former leaned

---

[28] Stoehr T., "Introduction aux essais psychologiques de Paul Goodman" in *Revue Gestalt*, number 3, autumn 1992, pp 59-73.

[29] Perls F., Hefferline R., Goodman P., *Gestalt Therapy; Excitement and Growth in the Human Personality*, New York, Julian Press, 1951.

towards methodology, efficiency, the confrontation of ideas. The latter was a philosopher, molded by literature, who looked for the nuance, the beauty of an idea. As Fritz suggested in his first work, they refused their introjections, that is, they confronted their ideas in a "healthy aggressiveness" until assimilation. Then they wrote the chapters without thinking any more about the sources of their thought.

This work ended by straining their friendship to the breaking point. Paul, however, remained very close to Laura. In the view of Joe Wysong, the long-time publisher of the *Gestalt Journal*, the manuscript was written in equal parts by Fritz and Paul; certain passages were improved, from Fritz's original heavily Germanic English. Others like Taylor Stoehr, Goodman's biograper and literary executor, think that Fritz's contribution was limited to only those pages written in South Africa.[30] But the exact origin of these writings may not be important, as they were, for the most part, a synthesis of the ideas which had been discussed by the "group of seven."

For Fritz, the book got off to a difficult start and the development of this new approach seemed too slow: So he, the eternal traveler, crossed the United States to set up small groups and promote his ideas. He met pioneers of other new therapies, and took up Zen. Each time he integrated what he learned into his art, such as the importance of bodily messages (muscular contractions, breathing), and the use of theatre in therapy (psychodrama).

In 1952, the Perlses founded the *New York Gestalt Institute*,[31] but Laura made it quite clear that she didn't want to teach there; her

---

[30] Robine J.M "Entretien avec Taylor Stoehr" in *Revue Gestalt*, number 3, autumn 1992, pp.130-142.

[31] In 2002 this institute celebrated fifty years of training, conferencing and holding study seminars.

private clients and her role as a mother took up all her time. Fritz was finally finished with twenty-three years of psychoanalytical practice. Forty students came to the first training seminar. Enough so that after some persuasion Laura accepted responsibility for half a group; that was the beginning of the teaching that she was to continue during her entire life. These first students were Perls' patients or friends of Goodman's. They were to become the pillars of the different American Institutes; for example, Isadore From, or Erving Polster.

The years of separation

Tension developed between Fritz, who felt that he was not appreciated enough, and the other members of the group, including Laura. In 1956, he gave up his position as director of the Institute and left for Miami on his own; she stayed in New York. A long term professional rivalry was born between Fritz, whom history has kept as the founder of Gestalt Therapy and Laura, who, with Goodman, developed first the New York Institute and then one in Cleveland. Fritz was crowned for his charisma in initiating and spreading this psychotherapy; Laura and Goodman had the work of developing the theory and training specialists.

"He never really left me," said Laura, "he was just absent from home for longer and longer."[32] Indeed, each time he stayed in New York, Laura welcomed him into her home. Fritz wrote his feelings about the cause of the distance between them: "I felt more and more ill-at-ease with Laura, who always made me feel inferior, and at that time, had nothing good to say about me. "[33]

In Miami, Fritz, who was now sixty-three, felt ill and depressed. He had very few clients. He tried some LSD, which was

---

[32] Shepard M., *Le Père de la Gestalt dans l'intimité de Fritz Perls, op. cit.*

[33] Perls F., *Ma Gestalt thérapie, une poubelle vue du dedans et du dehors, op. cit.*

fashionable in the anti-establishment circles at the time. Then he fell in love with Marty Fromm and his energy returned.

> *From the Jew hunted down in Holland, to the wealthy bourgeois in South Africa, to the "little boy," mortified at not having been better welcomed by Freud, to the revered guru, to the inexhaustible traveler always ready to question his life, to the bitter man of this period, Perls experienced a life full of extremes. He seemed to start his life all over again each day. His wife said of him "He's a prophet and a vagabond."[34]*

As for Goodman, he continued to pursue his many different interests. He taught at the University of Chicago, obtained his doctorate in 1954, and gave lectures throughout the country. A committed writer and journalist, openly homosexual (or bisexual), he detached himself little by little from psychotherapy and became one of the leaders of the young anti-establishment generation. He lost his job because of his open homosexuality, then edited the magazine *Complex*. When he published his book, *Growing Up Absurd*, in 1960, he was on the front cover of *Life* magazine. He extended the concepts developed in Gestalt Therapy, without referring to it specifically.

Like Fritz, he refused norms and conventions and criticized centralized government. He believed that the transformation of the world should come through the transformation of the individual: he gave psychology a social and political role by valuing the self-regulation of the individual or the group in their social environment and he preached a libertarian anarchism.[35] Susan Sontag wrote about him: "He was our Sartre, our Cocteau."[36]

---

[34] Perls L., *Vivre à la frontière, op. cit.*

[35] Goodman P., *Utopian Essays and Practical Proposals,* Vintage Books, New York 1962.

[36] Sontag S., (1972) *Sous le signe de Saturne,* Paris, Le Seuil, 1985.

Success

In 1959, Perls accepted the position of counselor in a psychiatric hospital in California and moved to Los Angeles where he built up a new practice. His approach was more and more recognized as a phenomenological experience which was neither religious like Buber's, nor verbal like Heidegger's, nor "communist" like Sartre's. [37]

In 1962, at the age of seventy, he went on an eighteen-month round-the-world tour, including Israel, where painting became his major preoccupation, and Japan, where he practiced Zen. For a while he thought about moving to Kyoto, a town he had fallen in love with. He also traveled to Europe, in particular to Rome where Otto Dix, [38] one of the Bauhaus painters, made a portrait of "Dr. Fritz Perls."

Then he decided to go home and spend some time in New York with Laura, and then set up home at Esalen, an international seminar center, halfway between Los Angeles and San Francisco. Many people went there every year for courses in yoga, therapy and massage. Esalen attracted people of both European and American origin, who were looking for a freer, more authentic life, during the huge libertarian and human potential movement which was to resonate in Europe in the revolutionary years around 1968.

Perls spent five years in Esalen, and it was a springboard for the fame he had long desired. He led therapy and training workshops, became one of the leading lights of the center. He compared Esalen with Bauhaus: "What Bauhaus was in Germany for the creation of a new style in architecture and the arts, Esalen is for a new development in humanist psychology."[39] During this

---

[37] Perls F., *A life chronology, op. cit.*

[38] This portrait is reproduced in the show catalogue of the painter: *Otto Dix: Metropolis,* Fondation Maeght, 06570 Saint-Paul-de-Vence, 1998, 270 p.

[39] Personal unedited notes by Perls.

period, there was a great focus on immediate experience and the search for one's own values. Gestalt Therapy gave sense, a theoretical-clinical cohesion, to what each individual felt the need to do, to feel, or to try.

His seductive and provocative temperament brought him both admiration and hostility. He was astonished to discover that one can "love oneself, hate oneself and still stay in one piece." His health improved, he gave lectures all over the country and visited Europe every year.

Gestalt Therapy was definitely emerging into the spotlight. In 1968 Fritz' photo made the cover of *Life* magazine, showing his long white beard and his guru-like appearance with laughing eyes; that photo brought him great renown. His gift for detecting in a few minutes someone's existential difficulties encouraged him to give demonstration workshops which attracted both beginners and specialists in human relationships, including Europeans.

Perls developed the technique of the *hot-seat:* the person who wants to "work" comes and sits opposite him on the "hot-seat" thereby showing his willingness to engage himself. In 1969, each conference-workshop attracted two to three hundred people. Some of the courses were taped onto videos and then published and distributed.[40] In his deliberately grandiloquent style which was appreciated by Americans at that time, he wrote, "My serenity, my humor and my therapeutic abilities increase in relation to my happiness."

The professional rivalry between Fritz and Laura became more evident. Fritz emphasized demonstration and training; he became widely known as "the guru of the here and now," an expression that he was quite happy with. He gradually distanced himself from the fundamental concepts developed in *Gestalt Therapy* and happily assimilated all the elements that he could glean from other

---

[40] Perls F., *Gestalt Therapy Verbatim,* La Fayette, Real People Press, 1969.

psychotherapists. Laura preferred a deeper approach to her work and stayed faithful to the specific nature of Gestalt psychotherapy.

Gestalt Therapy Verbatim

This book, published in 1969, was a collection of four interviews, several seminars on dreams, and an intensive course on his method. They were transcribed, sometimes verbatim from films or tapes. This approach is moving, because it allows the reader to witness Fritz's actual work, but also sometimes irritating in its style; there is a huge difference between the spoken and the written word. Some copies of the tapes and films are still available. This book, which was surprisingly called "*Rêves et existence en Gestalt-thérapie*,"[41] (or *Dreams and existence...*) when it came out in French. It helped to make its author famous.

In the interview, Perls comments on the existential roots of his approach and defines *anxiety* as "the gap between the now and the afterwards." This book is particularly famous as an illustration of Perls' work on dreams. He suggested studying dreams, not as the magic key to access the unconscious, but as scattered fragments of our personality, fragments that we can reconstitute like a jigsaw puzzle to find an understandable form, a gestalt. Each element of the dream represents its author and can be worked on as "unfinished business." He was opposed to interpretation, that is, a symbolic reading of the dream, given by the therapist. We will come back to this theme of dreams, in its clinical aspect, in the 6th chapter.

---

[41] Perls F., *Rêves et existence en Gestalt-thérapie,* Paris, Epi, 1972.

In and out the Garbage Pail

1969 was a fertile year in literary production as Fritz also published an autobiographical narrative.[42]

We know that Fritz liked this very personal book, that he had in fact started it as a personal journal without any plans to publish it: "I started to write about my life and it began to flow, partly as poetry."[43]

The author recounted his life and tried to extract some concepts from it, in opposition to those who construct a theory and want their existence to match it; he said what he lived instead of trying to live what he said.

When he found it difficult, Perls used a dialogue between:
• *Top-dog*, the leader (in a dog team), tyrannical and rigid;
• And *Under-dog*, rebellious and freedom-loving.

The eternal traveler

After five years at Esalen, Fritz decided to leave again... He wanted to create a community where he could "live Gestalt

---

[42] Perls F., *In and Out the Garbage Pail*, Moab, Real People Press, 1969; French translation: *Ma Gestalt-thérapie, une poubelle vue du dedans et du dehors, op. cit.*
[43] Words taken from a transcribed seminar in *Rêves et existences en Gestalt-thérapie.*

twenty-four hours a day." At the age of seventy-six (June 1969), he bought an old motel in Canada on Vancouver island and, with

a few friends, founded a new Gestalt Institute. Twenty to thirty residents attended therapy courses or came to be trained; all shared a life which was comparable to that of a *kibbutz*. Perls was happy in what he called his "family." The fighter no longer had to

battle to convince others, since he was surrounded by people who shared his ideas. He described himself as being at peace for the first time in his life.

He continued travelling to America, Europe and Japan, for conferences like the one in Chicago in 1970. However, when he got off the plane, he had a fever: seven hundred people were waiting for him at the university but the conference was cancelled at the last minute. Fritz went to the hospital and died there four days later, in his seventy-seventh year. His last words clearly reveal his personality: his body was riddled with tubes and he suddenly started to get up. When a nurse called out, "Dr. Perls, you mustn't get up!" he became furious: "I forbid you to tell me what I must do!" and then died.

Paul Goodman made the memorial speech at his funeral. After Fritz's death, the founding members of the group (particularly Laura and Paul) and their students continued the process of developing Gestalt Therapy, especially the theoretical bases, and made sure that it spread. The split between Fritz's students (actors in a therapy that was personally, bodily and emotionally engaging, and developed mainly on the west coast of the United States), and the students from the New York Institute (who concentrated more on the theory), has been largely forgotten today.

Isadore From, in particular, based his teaching on the detailed study of the theories of Goodman and trained a number of European Gestalt therapists. "It's all in the book," he was fond of saying, quoting *Gestalt Therapy: Excitement and Growth in the Human Personality.*

The impact of Gestalt is still greatly felt in the United States. Some also refer to a "west coast" or "east coast" style: this expression has crossed the Atlantic, to distinguish, in a sometimes outdated way, the differing approaches.

> *Gestalt Therapy had, as a founding father, a man who could not be idealized as a model. His married life was not satisfactory for very long and he was an absent father to his two children. His professional life was a strange mixture of brilliant intuitions and resounding failures.*
>
> *This frees up each Gestalt therapist, who doesn't have to identify with a "good image" which he might have to reproduce. It's the proof, yet again, that the therapist is not someone who has "sorted everything out in his own life" but someone who is constantly changing and seeking.*
>
> *What I retain of Perls, is his incredible vital energy, his remarkable intuition, his acceptance of the paradoxes in his life, and his insatiable curiosity… What I retain of Goodman, is the finesse of his theoretical analysis and his social activism in the service of a better world.*

All the founding members of the group have since died. Paul Goodman in 1972, Laura in 1990 at the age of eighty-five, Isadore From in 1993.

And in Europe

The implantation of European Gestalt Therapy first took place in Germany, where there are now several thousand professionals involved in psychotherapy, training, teaching, working in companies, etc.

In France in 1971, several psychotherapists (who knew very little of each other) were trained in the United States. They regularly proposed personal development courses based on Gestalt, thus preparing the way for the development of Gestalt psychotherapy in France.

The two volumes of *Gestalt Therapy* were translated into a number of languages and published in Quebec in 1977 and 1979.[44] The Quebec Gestalt Center began training French-speaking professionals in Europe, in 1979. It was the start of a long story which we will develop in the third part of this book, after having studied the principal concepts of this psychotherapeutic approach.

---

[44] Perls F., Hefferline R., Goodman P., (1951) French translation *Gestalt-thérapie*. Montreal, Stanke, 1977 and 1979.

A THERAPY OF THE
HERE AND NOW

A new approach

Preliminary remarks

Before detailing the principal theoretical concepts, I would like to present a synthesis of what the Gestalt approach is, because "the whole is different from the sum of its parts."

I wrote in the introduction that Gestalt is, first of all, **a place of welcome**. It was a place of welcome right from the start, as we have seen with the "group of seven"—that group which was in itself very eclectic and met regularly at the Perls' home. In addition, the book setting out the basics of Gestalt Therapy was written by three very different people. And finally, it was launched in the United States by Paul Goodman, Fritz and Laura Perls, who all had very different styles. To my knowledge, Gestalt is the only therapy which does not depend on a single charismatic personality: for example Freud for psychoanalysis, Berne for transactional analysis, Reich for the body therapies, etc. Each person comes to Gestalt Therapy with his or her own sensitivity and centers of interest.

Every therapeutic movement rests on several principles which seem indispensable: a concept of good psychological **health** (and therefore also, psychopathology), a **philosophical base**, and a **strategy of intervention**. We are therefore going to approach the idea of health, then explore Gestalt's therapeutic strategy by studying the fundamental concepts along with their existential roots, and finally, discuss the style of intervention.

Health and psychopathology

The idea of good health in Gestalt Therapy seems to be very close to the definition put forward by the World Health Organization: "Health is not merely the absence of illness or infirmity but rather, a complete state of physical, mental and social well-being."

Goodman insists on the idea that health includes several components: physical, psychological and cultural. The idea of health and pathology in the Gestalt approach seems to me to be fundamentally **phenomenological**,[45] that is, it is not the truth of my situation that is important, but the echo of that situation within me. It is **my** awareness of an event that gives it meaning.

Phenomenology is both an experimental method and a philosophical movement developed by Husserl[46]. Phenomenology tries to describe, rather than explain, observable facts. It means avoiding "a discourse about things," and returning to "the thing itself as it is lived," avoiding interpretation.[47] As soon as I abandon this phenomenological approach, I begin to make judgments about others.

When I meet a client, my viewpoint is clouded by my "intention," that is, it is directed "towards something"—for example, understanding, remembering or loving. I "go towards" my clients in the same way as "they come towards" me. The concept of intention takes into account this double movement.

---

[45] From the Greek *phainein* "to lighten" or *phenomeina* "celestial constellation" and *logos* "the word."

[46] Edmund Husserl (1859-1938), German philosopher, father of phenomenology.

[47] Kunzmann P. et al, *Atlas de la philosophie*, Paris, Livre de Poche 1993.

Phenomenology seeks to highlight this subjectivity. Pheno-menological psychology seeks less to explain than to understand human beings.[48]

> *I use an example which is a long way from therapy to explain what I mean: the study of a television set. An electrician would describe it in terms of transistors, power supply, the quality of the cathode tube. An artist would describe it in terms of color and form; a businessperson in terms of price and competition. As a therapist I come to a television in relational terms: what matters to me is to observe if family conversations are interrupted when the television is switched on, how children eat when they are watching their favorite serial, etc. The same television set is therefore the object of a thousand different observations, depending on the intention of the person interacting with it.*

The concept of psychopathology in the Gestalt process is phenomenological in approach. It cannot be only didactic, that is, turned towards the identification of an illness or a symptom. It is, moreover, relational, temporal and contextual, as I will try to explain below.

• **Relational**—because an individual is never a carrier of suffering on his own. That suffering appears in a certain type of relationship with other people.

> *Francoise,[49] for example, one of my very first clients, is not hysterical when she is on her own. She develops this tendency in therapy and in contact with me. I am a man, our difference in age means that I could well be her father, her long journey in therapy has developed her creative and seductive potential; all these elements act upon the relationship and*

---

[48] Sillamy N., *Dictionnaire usuel de psychologie*, Paris, Bordas 1983.

[49] All clients' names have been changed to protect confidentiality.

> *therefore affect the way "my gaze rests on her," in psychopathological terms.*[50]

• **Temporal and contextual** : that is, an individual's way of "being in the world" changes depending on the moment and the context.

> *So Francoise, after a day at work where her extraverted attitude helps her in her commercial job, goes on to develop a tendency to be more closed-in on herself in her family life. This allows her to "regain her strength" or calms her agitation by means of a certain obsession which she expresses by stamp collecting (she only collects red or blue animal stamps!)*

In the Gestalt approach, psychopathology is considered to be a rigidity which blocks the process of growth, a maladjustment to an environment, which is in a state of perpetual change. We insist on the principle of uniqueness, that is to say that each of us develops his or her original way of adjusting to the world. This can be frustrating for those who look for general rules to describe human behavior.

An original therapeutic strategy

The idea of "therapeutic strategy" is fundamental and innovative in Gestalt Therapy. It seems to me to rest on three concepts: **dialogue, hermeneutics,** and **process**. It is the combination of these three strategies that make the Gestalt approach so original and relevant.

---

[50] So I am choosing not to use the word "diagnosis."

A model of dialogue

In a book published in 1923, the philosopher Martin Buber[51] offered two opposing concepts which he called the "basic words": "I-Thou" and "I-It" which are two ways of being in the world and especially, of conducting relationships. I will develop here only that which concerns the helping relationship.

• The medical model proposes an **I-It** relationship. The doctor (I) observes the illness (It) which shows through certain symptoms. His skill lies in finding a good diagnosis, since writing a prescription is easy: if the diagnosis is right, then the medicine is "responsible" for fighting the illness. The only responsibility the patient has is to find the doctor and follow the prescription. Traditional medicine is built on this scientific model. The medicine and the "bacteria" take center stage.

• In the **I-Thou** relationship, two different human beings, one a professional and the other a client, establish a contact of dialogue and it is that relationship which is healing. "In the beginning is the relationship," wrote Buber. The symptom is then considered as a language or an appeal for help, a difficulty in relationships which prevents the person from developing his full potential.

Goodman is both close to and radically different from Martin Buber. Both of them share an anthropological vision of Man as one who exists through the relationships he builds. A person without contact is nothing. But Buber developed a philosophical and spiritual approach *(How to develop the quality of relationships with others and with God)* while Goodman put himself in a cultural and social perspective *(Let us change society to change Man)*.

Perls was also inspired by this basic idea that he applied to therapy. Moreover, his wife Laura had been a student of Buber's

---

[51] Buber M (1923), trad. franc, *Je et Tu*, Paris, éditions Aubier, 1969.

in Vienna. One may speak then of a therapy of dialogue in which the hyphen of the I-Thou is in the spotlight.

This model of the I-Thou is an idea which we approach and which gets put into place gradually. Indeed, our society is impregnated by the I-It model and a patient often relies on this function at the beginning of therapy by saying things like, "Tell me what I have to do." We need therefore to adapt, to accommodate to his or her expectations (but not too much), so that confidence is established (what we call the "therapeutic alliance") and to allow the dialogue model to establish itself. This will take time and may include periods of fragility.

> *Marie comes to "consult" with me because she is having difficulties with her only daughter, who is an adolescent. On the telephone she called me Doctor... She is always asking me for advice and puts her faith in the fact that I have four children of my own and so must have plenty of experience...*
>
> *She takes several months to realize that I can't help her through my comments, but that I can listen to her suffering and teach her to be "in a relationship" without suffocating the other person. She underlines this in her language and moves from "I am doing therapy" to "I'm in therapy."*

The therapeutic alliance of Gestalt Therapy supposes that the client experiences therapy as bringing help and support (the affective alliance) and that an atmosphere of co-operation is created. Client and therapist have the feeling of a common objective (the work alliance). And as Buber affirmed, "once the moment of meeting has passed, a man does not emerge the same as when he entered."

A hermeneutic approach

When people ask me about my choice of Gestalt as opposed to other movements that I have known, I always quote the qualifier of *hermeneutics* as a basis for my motivation. What does the word mean?

In ancient Greek, it meant "making understood." In Diderot's *Encyclopaedia* (1747), it designated "the art of discovery of the exact meaning of a text."[52] Modern hermeneutics insists on the idea that the study itself of a text can bring a multiplicity of meanings and interpretations that is **polysemy.**

Gestalt is *hermeneutic* because it doesn't pretend to bring one single interpretation to an event. We return to the contribution of Martin Buber: there is no longer a professional, given the job of making sense of the material brought by the client. It is from the search through dialogue that the image is going to emerge, that is, the meaning of what the client is working on in therapy. At the beginning of the session this form is **hidden from both partners.**[53]

It appears gradually like those black and white photos that I used to plunge into the revealing fluid when I was an adolescent.

> *Eric has been talking to me about blackness, about storms, about conflict since the beginning of the session. In his eyes everything is despair. And yet, during our work, a question about what really attaches him to life, brings the answer of a yacht which only needs a captain... Playing with the waves, calculating the wind, getting out the storm sails, that is one way of rediscovering pleasure.*

---

[52] *Le Robert: dictionnaire historique de la langue française*, Paris, Robert, 1998.
[53] In old French, "partner" meant the person you danced with!

The Gestalt therapist is therefore different from other professionals "who are supposed to know" and whose interpretations are aimed at helping the "patient" to better understand what is happening. This approach often surprises new clients, who, through their rather naïve questions ("Tell me what it means?"), want us to give them a diagnosis, a ready-made solution for their difficulties.

Perls liked to repeat that for him, every interpretation is a therapeutic mistake, and that it is important that the image emerges by itself!

> *Therapists don't often speak of their jubilation. I sometimes feel intense pleasure, a deep joy, when a new way emerges from the fog during a session of work. We go forward like blind men, drowning in a landscape of fears, resistances, blocked by difficulties that seem insurmountable.*
>
> *Then gradually a new landscape appears and we discover an unexpected path. My client's face lights up, my heart sings, a blocked process begins to move.*

When I explain this fundamental notion to therapists in training, one question always comes up. "So would this same client, through another therapist, have found a different meaning to his difficulties?" I answer in the affirmative and I find that reassuring: that is the richness of polysemy.

Focusing on the process

Some types of therapy are centered on the cause and search for the origins of trauma. These are "therapies of discovery;" psychoanalysis is the prototype, but it is not the only one. "Primal scream" or rebirthing techniques try to rediscover the trauma of birth; Reichian therapy undoes the knots of muscular armor to release suppressed pain which is inscribed in the body.

Other approaches are the "support therapies" which put the origins of our blockages to one side. These therapies seek to free up the behavior, to "unblock the river" and "clear the banks" to allow it to flow more freely. Behavioral therapies use this strategy.

Continuing the water metaphor, Gestalt is a "therapy of the current"; what is important is the flow of the river, in other words **how** it flows (calmly, flooding, etc.) rather than why. We are trying to reactivate that which our past, education or trauma has rigidified in our psyche, like a rock in the river. This concentration on the process (a Latin word which means progress, progression) is found in the vocabulary in the following chapter. I like the dynamic resonance of the vocabulary: the contact-boundary, "unfinished business," the breaking of contact.

In terms of the process, Gestalt Therapy modifies the axis of time: the difficulty is examined in the framework of **the here and now**. This is a very powerful idea developed by Perls when he separated himself from psychoanalysis: namely that it is impossible to relive an original traumatic event, which has been modified by memory. The exactness of the facts is not fundamental because the context has changed. What is real is that I have been living for several years with this wound: the emotion emerges in the present, even though it is rooted in the past.

Perls also insists on the "how and now" to shed light on the process. It is not helpful to reconstitute the whole history of the subject, because "today" is when the conflict is occurring, especially in the body and the emotions. By associating phenomenology, that is to say the uniqueness of his experience, with the "how and now," the client discovers his existential immediacy.

> *If, for example, I concentrate on a difficulty of my childhood, I won't speak about it in the past tense. If I decide to work on my present sadness ("Dad, I'm sad today because you abandoned me") or if I decide to put myself into the context of my youth and to relive the scene ("Dad, I'm sad because you are abandoning me") I can evoke my pain in the here and now.*
>
> *We value emotion in the present, so as to find the best adjustment possible in relation to a given situation, which we can probably not change.*

What an expressive word "now" is! My life in the present is what I have "in my hands" now: my past is irremediably lived, my future is uncertain. As for "here," it is both an adverb of place and an adverb of time (from here until tomorrow, for example).

A three-part waltz

It might be reductive to give a typical example of a session of Gestalt Therapy especially having insisted on the dialogic and phenomenological aspects of the approach. Nevertheless I am going to take that risk. In this process, we develop an **experiential strategy**. In a "typical" session whether at an individual or group level, we can most often identify three phases:

• The client brings either a difficulty or a present feeling; the therapist helps him to involve himself (the existential stance of **freedom** and **responsibility**) and to concentrate on the feeling in the here and now (awareness). Through his qualites of listening and openness of heart, the therapist seeks to establish the therapeutic alliance, within an I-Thou relationship.

• Then he builds with the client an **experimentation**, with the goal of developing creativity, of shedding a new light on the difficulty being worked on, of discovering a hidden emotion. This experimentation invites the client to change his "habits of contact" with the environment. This approach is hermeneutic, that is, no one knows in advance the image that will emerge from this acting out. The therapist is then often an "obstetrician of emotion": the feelings are there, hidden; they are asking to emerge, to rediscover their freedom; but the "birth" mustn't be too brutal, or there is a risk of damage. Time must be given to time. Rushing is a classic mistake of the professional at the beginning of his career.

• The third stage is that of **assimilation**, that is, the creation of links between what has been discovered in the protected framework of a session and the realities of the outside world, which have not necessarily changed. This time of assimilation lengthens outside the session and gives the therapy a guideline, that of progress towards a greater freedom. The therapist must resist an eventual request by the client (and indeed his own need of "taking over") of giving his own solutions.

In order for these different stages to take place correctly, the therapist has several obligations: a profound personal therapy, so that he may have himself lived through this adventure, serious training to acquire the theoretical signposts, regular supervision by a more experienced peer in order to sort out at regular intervals what belongs to him alone and could encumber the client, and finally, adherence to a strict code of professional ethics, which guarantees the framework of therapy.

The principal concepts

By way of prelude to the theory...

We are in a pretty, large room, a little strange though, with a ceiling the color of the sky decorated with little white clouds. We've come for a three-day residential Gestalt course. Three days of intensive work, where each person can explore personal fears, blockages, desires and frustrations, at his or her own pace.

At the moment, Catherine "is working"—which means that she has asked for some time, time when the therapist and the whole group will help her to shed light on the difficulty she has brought to the group.

Catherine is gentle and pretty. At this time, she is crying and expressing, in a few measured words, her anger with her parents. We are seated in a circle on large cushions, and I am facing her.

She says, "My father was too hard, he thought he was doing the right thing, bringing us up right, but he broke us and blocked us."

I am not trying to really understand the meaning of the words, I'm just letting myself be impregnated with the huge anger and deep despair which seem to paralyze her. I avoid asking her "Who" or "Why" questions which would "send her back into her head" and make her lose the thread of her emotions; I simply feed back to her what I observe.

Me: "you're not breathing any more?" She looks at me with huge, frightened eyes, stifles a sob and then, silently, dissolves into tears.

> *Me: "Is there anyone here who can represent your father? " Catherine chooses without the least hesitation a course member who is younger than herself, whose body is a bit stiff. She later said that at that moment he had the hard look of her father.*

Our projections (that is, the images which belong to us but which we "project" onto another person) are often so powerful that they don't stop at certain contradictions of age or gender, for example, but concentrate on a global form, which "takes the stand" by coming to the forefront.

> *Me: "Can you speak to him? "*
>
> *Catherine: "Why did you do that? You had no right; I was scared, you could have killed **him**!"*
>
> *Me: "You're talking in a tiny voice; and you are still not breathing properly. Can you tell you father again what he had no right to do?"*
>
> *I still don't know **who** the father might have killed. I am concentrating on her voice and her breathing, because I have noticed that Catherine's work is blocking my own breathing and that the whole group seems to be hanging on her breath.*

In Gestalt, we call this awareness, the vigilance of what we have lived through physically and emotionally; in this case, my own breathing has alerted me to what is being played out in front of us.

> *Catherine, after several clumsy efforts, finally expresses her anger and her fear. Her lungs seem suddenly to open and unblock themselves: a great in-breath gives her back all her vitality. Her eyes brighten.*

We call these magical moments *insight* when an idea, an image or a feeling appears and suddenly feel clear and luminous. This insight suddenly appears more easily in an emotional, surprising, unusual context. Often the group amplifies this climate.

The whole group relaxes. The spectacular phase, which has lasted about twenty minutes, seems to be at an end. I'm still not exactly sure which fear Catherine is working on, what is motivating her emotion. I have accompanied her, helped her to amplify her gestures, to dare to find her voice. During the feedback, that is, the space where those who want to can say what they have felt, Catherine gives us the key to what happened. She thought, at first, she was exploring her relationship with an authoritarian father, but without any precise direction.

My simple observation "you're not breathing" in an important emotional context, allowed a traumatic memory to resurface: her father had held her younger brother's head under a cold tap to calm him down. And she, the big sister, had been petrified, fearing that she would see him drown and felt guilty about not reacting.

Catherine is not a beginner. She is very familiar with therapy and was able to bounce off this memory herself, hidden deep in her emotional brain. Her asthma attacks happened regularly, each time that she was confronted with a refusal, an impossibility, an action which she couldn't finish... and the awareness of "how she stopped herself from breathing" in those situations, finally allowed her to clear up her asthma.

As a Gestalt therapist, I didn't work on the behavior or the symptom, but on the contact process between Catherine and her environment: how, with her father (as with oxygen), she stopped herself from living (breathing).

This example is neither magical nor empirical but rests on concepts which have the dual advantage of being both simple and practical. We are now going to examine what seems to me to be the pillars of Gestalt theory and which give this art a clear vision: the cycle of contact, the main resistances, the contact-boundary, the self and its functions, creative adjustment, awareness, healthy aggressiveness and polarities.

The contact cycle

This cycle describes the stages that we generally follow when we make contact with another person, a need within us, or an emotion.

What is involved is the cycle of contact-retreat, that is, the way in which a need emerges from our consciousness, develops and is satisfied, and then fades, to be replaced by a new need: at least that is the ideal unfolding process. So, while I am writing this article, the "dominant figure" is the intellectual pleasure I feel in putting my ideas into words. But if a twinge in my back tells me I am not sitting properly and becomes more painful, the physical sensation will become dominant; the writing will stop, unfinished, and I will stand up to relax: thus a new cycle of need will unfold, which I hope will not itself be interrupted by, for example, a telephone call.

Goodman[54] emphasized four principal phases of contact:

• **Pre-contact**: in the permanent flux of my sensations, of my needs, a precise stimulus suddenly becomes the figure which demands my interest: this stimulus detaches itself from the background, like an actor who moves center stage. This is the emergence of a new need.

• **Contacting**: is the active phase during which I choose to satisfy this need; I mobilize my energy to move into action. In my example, I choose to get up and walk about to take care of my back.

• **Full contact**: during this phase, I am in harmony with my needs: there is coherence between my perception, my choice and my actions.

• **Post-contact**: is the phase of retreat; my need is satisfied, I "digest" my actions and will become available for a new form, or to finish what I momentarily interrupted.

In a healthy person, these cycles happen in a permanent movement which is a source of growth. A need generates a tension; when this need is satisfied, the organism returns to a relaxed state... It's an adaptive phenomenon, indispensable to life, known by the term *homeostasis*.[55] When this mechanism no longer works, for example through an excess of stimulation, stress occurs with all its psychosomatic characteristics.

---

[54] Perls F., Hefferline R.,Goodman P., *Gestalt Therapy, op. cit.*

[55] From the Greek *homeos* "similar," and *stasis* "position." Homeostasis designates the organism's tendency to keep its conditions of equilibrium constant.

The therapist must be attentive to the unfolding process of these stages of satisfaction of needs and spot the blockages, the stops, the repetitions and the jumps. In practice, many contact figures are unsatisfactory. Often this "unfinished business" can be assimilated, because it doesn't bring any intolerable frustration.

But sometimes, an aborted gestalt, that is, a cycle where we were unable to live through the resolution, remains like an open wound and blocks our energy, preventing us from letting homeostasis have free rein. It is the repetition of disturbances of the operation of the cycle that should draw our attention.

Perls defined a *neurotic* as "a person who chronically repeats self-interruption."[56] He invited us to constantly stay in touch with lived experience. The state of tension provoked by incomplete cycles can block the development of the human being and his ability to adapt to his environment. The compulsive repetition of a situation is directed towards life, in the hope of finishing a blocked gestalt, in order to free up the energy and again take up the process of growth.

> *Val has been in individual therapy for six months. What strikes me about her, is her inability to enter into "full contact" with what she does or the people she meets. She is always elsewhere... She thinks about Peter when she is with Paul, always regrets what she hasn't done, changes activity all the time. This avoidance, of course, comes up during therapy: she changes the subject as soon as I encourage her to explore the theme that she has brought up, she always keeps a distance from her emotions, and avoids contact with me, the male therapist.*
>
> *I need "an iron fist in a velvet glove" to allow her gradually to enter into full contact with her needs and to stay there. By learning, during a session, not to change the direction, to explore a feeling right to the end*

---

[56] Perls F., *Rêves et existence en Gestalt-therapie, op. cit.*

> *even if it is disagreeable, like her anger at her mother or her disgust for men, Val develops her capacity for full contact.*
>
> *A clear sign shows me that she is making progress: now, she finishes her sessions without anxiety, and her "good-byes" are no longer drawn out; satisfied by a time of full contact, she no longer has a need to beg for an extension of time.*

I have illustrated Goodman's "full contact" with the example of Val, but other cycle models have been put forward by different authors. When they are too detailed, they lose their practical use, that is, they no longer allow an indicator during the session itself. One variant, though, seems to me to be of interest: that which was put forward by Serge Ginger,[57] emphasizing the periods of engagement and withdrawal.

Engagement is the time where the action is brought to a head: in therapy, it's the time where the direction of work is clarified, where the client and the therapist decide to explore one area rather than another. This moment is sometimes clearly noted ("so let's begin shall we?") or sometimes implicit.

The time of disengagement is often a critical and difficult moment to get through; it can be at the end of a session, but also at the end of therapy itself. How and when should we engage in this process of "withdrawal" which is a prelude to the period of assimilation?

---

[57] Ginger S., *La Gestalt : l'art du contact,* Marabout, Bruxelles, 1955, 4° édition 2000.

- The Contact cycle (in five steps) -

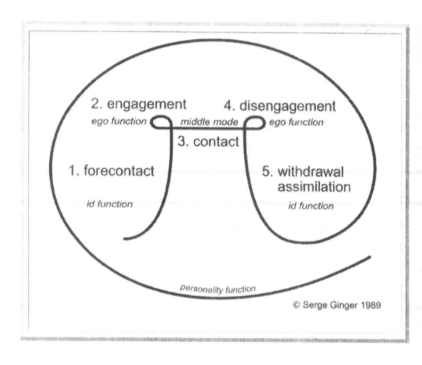

2. engagement   4. disengagement
ego function *middle mode* *ego function*
3. contact

1. forecontact   5. withdrawal
                     assimilation

id function   *id function*

personality function

© Serge Ginger 1989

Matthew's relationships are chaotic. At forty, he's on his own : "I have a fine scoreboard of affairs, but not one of them wants to stay with me," he says with lassitude. From affair to affair, little by little he is entering a solitude full of resentment against women. His difficulty? He is always out of sync with his partners in the unfolding of the cycle of contact. He is:

- either too quick in the pre-contact phase and chases women away in the moment of engagement;

- or he runs away: he withdraws too quickly and generates aggressiveness.

> *As for the phase of assimilation, he systematically avoids it in order not to feel the suffering of solitude. A relationship bulimia takes place, which makes girlfriends run away and the vicious circle is continued.*

So we are talking about the repeated breaking of the contact cycle; I would however like to emphasize that the idea of "seeing a cycle through to the end" is not an end in itself.

As Bluma Zeigarnick[58] showed in 1927, in an experiment since regarded as classic, that an unfinished task leaves an important trace in the memory. She asked children to finish about twenty practical tasks in a day: some could be finished and others not. A week later, the unfinished tasks were remembered twice as often as the others. This "Zeigarnick effect" is often used by the media for example, when the "advertising break" comes at a key moment in a soap opera!

It may be wise to stop as soon as the pre-contact phase is reached, that is, not to engage in action when the environment is not right or because the need could harm others, because new priorities are emerging etc. Education, for example, is an apprenticeship of not fulfilling desires as soon as they emerge.

The principal resistances

The cycle does not always unfold according to a simple plan. It is precisely the difficulties in unfolding, the ruptures (which we call "resistances") which are often the most significant.

---

[58] A Russian psychologist, who was a student of Gestalt theory with Kurt Lewin.

Let's look at the main resistances[59] which disturb the unfolding of the contact cycle:

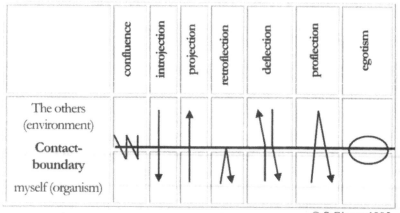

© S.Ginger 1985

• **Confluence:** in this resistance, there is no longer any difference between myself and my environment. The needs that emerge are not mine. Confluence blocks the contact cycle, by not allowing a personal figure to emerge in the pre-contact phase; it also prevents access to the time of retreat, which is indispensable to assimilation and to the emergence of a new figure.

> *In a couple, one person with a confluent tendency often speaks in the plural "we have problems with our children; we want to repaint the kitchen, etc." This type of person has great difficulty with "ends of cycles," that is, the necessary period of taking a distance before the sharing of a new action, as I evoked with Val in a preceding example.*

Please note that all these resistances also have a healthy form. Pathology appears when the mechanisms come into play in a

---

[59] Note that the term "resistance" is used in a different way in psychoanalysis: there, it designates everyhing which shows up during a therapy as a break on its unfolding.

maladaptive or repetitive way, because they block the fluid unfolding of the cycle of contact-retreat. Momentary confluence is one of the pleasures of a love life, whether it is during a honeymoon or the sexual act, etc.

• **Introjection**: if I am content with "swallowing without chewing," I may have within me undigested foreign elements. Introjection, therefore, means swallowing "whole" ideas and principles which will distort the perception of real needs. This is the domain of dictums such as: "you must," "you must not," "all you need to do is…"

Uncovering unnecessary introjections helps us not to throw ourselves into dissatisfying actions and therefore, not to expend our energy in containing foreign bodies.

> *George, a brilliant company manager, feels the need, every night, to be the last to leave the office. One session was centered on the theme of "how he allows his agenda to overflow." This focus gave him the chance to uncover an introjection: his father, also a company manager, passed on the model of the captain who is the last to leave his ship; "chewing over the introjection" allows him not to be systematically the last to leave the office, but rather, to choose to be the first to arrive, which better matches his biorhythms and makes him more efficient.*

> *It is not therefore a question of destroying an idea which suits him (a manager works hard) but rather of modifying an irrelevant introjection (I must be the last to leave the office) as a function of a biological reality (I like getting up early).*

My literary choice of illustrating these theoretical points with clinical cases presents the risk of shedding light on the therapeutic "events" while leaving the process in shadow, that is, the slow alchemy which deeply alters a person's psyche. For George, for example, what is interesting is not that he changed his life rhythm, because a course on time management would have helped him just as much, but rather, that he should learn to detect his introjections and only keep those which suit him.

In fact, education depends in part on introjections, but the healthy adult has digested those principles which were inculcated during childhood: the healthy person examines an idea before adopting it, just as an epicure will bite and chew an apple before swallowing it. A momentary introjection is therefore indispensable in any type of education and apprenticeship necessarily passes through a time of imitation. This is the healthy form of introjection.

• **Projection**: this is the opposite of introjection. It consists in attributing to the environment elements which in fact come from the self.

> *So I can shorten this chapter, "so the reader doesn't become bored," when it is in fact myself who is tired. Projections falsify my adaptation to my environment and inhibit my creativity. For example, if I believe that my partner is in a bad mood today, then I may become aggressive towards her.*

Healthy projection, that is, non-invasive projection, is indispensable to be able to understand the other, by trying to put myself in his place. Intuition is a form of projection which can at times be "exactly right."

• **Retroflection:** this consists in doing to oneself as one would like to do to others.

> *For example, I bite my lip rather than verbally attacking my interlocutor.*

This interruption of the contact cycle, when it is repeated too often, is an open door to all sorts of psychic difficulties. We also use the term "retroflection" when we do to ourselves what we don't find around us.

> *I caress my face when I'm talking to a person from whom I'd like to receive tenderness, or I show off when I would like my interlocutor to think well of me.*

• **Deflection**: this is a particular form of retroflection which consists in redirecting my energy from its primary target: this is an avoidance maneuver.

> *So I prefer to break an ashtray rather than directly expressing my anger or, without meaning to, I have an accident in the company car rather than expressing my real difficulties with my manager.*

It can be a good move to doodle with frustration on a bit of paper (*deflection*) or to bite my nails (*retroflection*) rather than to vent my anger at my boss. These are yet again healthy forms of resistance.

The Gestalt practitioner, whether a psychotherapist or a management consultant, is therefore sometimes an economist who observes the border, records the imports and exports; he's sometimes a customs officer who tries to prevent the introduction of prohibited goods (*introjection*), sometimes a politician who seeks to open borders if they are too tight or to close them if they are too loose (*confluence*) and who establishes alliances with neighboring countries (*contactboundary*).

The contact-boundary

This concept seems to me to be one of the most interesting in the Gestalt approach. The contact-boundary is the place where exchanges take place, where *awareness* develops. A metaphor for this exchange might be the skin.

- this tissue is first a container: it gives form and limits our bodies, and a wound to the skin can bring about hemorrhaging or infection, etc.;
- the skin is also a place of exchange: we breathe through it, we eliminate toxins through sweat, etc.;
- the skin transmits sensual information: temperature, touch, etc. For example, it can transmit pleasure or disgust;
- the skin is not just external: in the form of tissues, it makes up the organs, limits the air or food inside us, etc.

So the contact-boundary is not just a boundary "between" which separates, but rather, a zone of exchange which both contains the organism and at the same time, touches the environment. However, the metaphor of the skin has its limitations, because in fact, the contact-boundary is a virtual place, a space which develops between myself and others, but also inside myself, between my lungs and the oxygen that I breathe, between my emotions and myself.

We cannot disassociate an organism from its environment. I can't make contact with my client without taking into account his social environment and also the established relationship between us. We use the term "field" for the indivisible entity of an organism in its environment at a given moment. It's the tissue of relationships, whether conscious or not, in which a person is placed. This field of organism-environment is the Gestalt psychotherapy workplace.

> *Claudia has been in therapy with me for two years, but for several months I have been feeling that we are no longer making progress; the trust and the therapeutic alliance seem to have changed. We have been looking for the reasons without success.*
>
> *It is a verbal slip which puts me on track; in a sequence where she is describing her current depression, she uses the formal "vous" to address me, whereas she had been using the informal "tu" for a long time. I*

emphasize this sudden distance on her part; she then realizes that a recent and violent conflict with her boss, has been interfering in our therapeutic relationship. I am the head of the Parisian Gestalt School: a "boss" cannot be welcoming, he must be exploitative. The contact-boundary between Claudia and myself has therefore shrunk, been disturbed, and tainted with suspicion, because of my hierarchical status.

It will take several sessions to "clean" these projections, for her to realize that the client-therapist relationship is different from the secretary-boss relationship, in short, for the organism-environment field to become again the realm of change and for the psychotherapy to continue its course.

In this example, the field is made of not only the therapeutic relationship "here and now," but also of the professional conflict, of the transference and counter-transference, etc. The Gestalt therapist therefore works on the contact, as I did with Claudia, that is, on what is exchanged between others and herself, between her own needs and herself, between the world and herself. The therapist tries to shed light on this contact, to make it more fluid, to allow richer and more diverse exchanges.

The self

The points that we have just looked at, that is, the contact cycle, resistances and the contact-boundary are the elements of a more global concept which we call *the theory of the self*.[60] This theory occupies a very strange place in the conception of Gestalt Therapy. It is central and fundamental but at the same time it is an impossible theory to define or get hold of, at least in simple terms.

---

[60] The French translator of *Gestalt Therapy* kept the term *self*, others prefer the translation *soi*. These two terms can sometimes lead to confusion (Winnicott's *self* or Jung's *Self* for example).

"To understand Gestalt, you need to read this book, but to understand this book, you need to know Gestalt," Perls and Goodman specified in their introduction to *Gestalt Therapy*.

The place of the self in Gestalt Therapy is adapted according to its practitioners; the "Goodmanites" put it center stage, the "Perlsians" use it less explicitly, at least in their daily practice.

So what is this famous "self"? Well, it's a process, a way of being in the world. It is therefore an untouchable entity, which one cannot freeze in order to study it. I specified in the introduction that Gestalt Therapy has taken us from the era of photography to cinema.[61]

The self is made up of the whole of the contact-boundary exchanges. I can therefore say of the self:

• that it unfolds, if the exchanges are frequent in a given situation;

• that it is maladjusted, if the exchanges are poor or stereotyped;

• that it is disturbed, if the resistances are too numerous and regularly interrupt the cycle.

The self is therefore, by definition, in perpetual movement. It is the way of being at each instant; it is made up of exchanges which take place at the contact-boundary between the self and the environment. The individual has an effect on the world, just as the world has an effect on the individual.

It was Goodman who developed this theory most completely in the second volume of *Gestalt Therapy*. He defined it as "the system of contacts." A self unfolds in a given field, which evolves according to context, to time: the self doesn't unfold in the same

---

[61] Goodman writes the word *Self* with a capital letter in *Gestalt Therapy*, but Perls suggests in *Dreams and Existence* that one ought to spell it with the lower case, to emphasise the idea that it is only a system of contact. I am now referring to this suggestion.

way in a family situation or a professional one. Through our contact-boundary work, through our vigilance of the process, through our watching the contact cycle and its various interruptions, we can help clients to find a more mobile self, which is better adapted to their various needs.

The three functions of the self

If we look at the self as a way of being in contact with the world, we can observe its intensity but also its style, that is, the "how" of our contact-boundary exchanges. We can better understand the functions of the self by connecting them to the contact cycle.

• The first mode of the self is the *id-function*. This mode is essentially **passive**, that is, I am not responsible for what emerges: "it just happens to me." These can be bodily sensations (I'm thirsty, I'm tired), conscious or unconscious needs which are imposed on me. This mode intervenes in the beginning of the contact cycle and it is generally fleeting. It can be fragmented and seem incoherent, when I am bombarded by multiple needs.

• The *personality-function* is more **stable**. It is fed by my experience and my history. It makes up the basis of who I am or more precisely who I think I am. It is this function of the self which allows me to be enriched by experience. It is therefore permanent in any relationship with the world, in all stages of the cycle: this is what forges my identity and allows me to grow through the process of assimilation.

• The *ego-function* is that of **choice**, of the affirmation of what I want. I make decisions on the basis of what I feel (the id-function) and of my experience (personality-function). This way of being is therefore essentially **active**: I am conscious of acting; of interacting. These three functions are different from the Freudian concepts of Id, Ego and Super-Ego, or of the Jungian concepts of

Self, in that they are not fixed structures or psychic demands, but ways of relating to the world.

Ownership of the self

Goodman insists on the fact that the self develops spontaneously and in the **middle mode**. In French we don't conjugate verbs in this mood. The Greeks use this grammatical form for verbs that are neither active nor passive, but require an interaction. For example "to fight" is a middle mode, because it implies an adversary: the two protagonists are engaged in the same combat. This idea in French is often translated by a pronoun. This "middle mode" is principally developed at the moment of **full contact**, that is, when a person is engaged in action.

The disturbances of the functions of the self

It is the disturbances of the functions of the self which are the object of therapy:

• The **id-function** is disturbed when a person loses touch with his sensations and needs. In a psychotic condition, access is interrupted, in a neurotic condition it is altered. The person therefore loses his sources of information. The other functions (personality and ego) will therefore unfold according to false bases.

> *Natalie was a victim of incest in her childhood. Gradually she cut herself off from all physical feelings. She mentions during therapy that she doesn't feel desire or pleasure, in sexual terms as in all other bodily aspects: she is unable to feel the quality of a meal, the beauty of a landscape, or the poetry in a song. Without an id-function, the personality cannot enrich itself and therapy can't*

"anchor itself." Natalie took several months to relearn to accept herself as a "desiring and desirable person," in her own words.

• When the **personality-function** is perturbed, the individual develops a false perception of who he is. Introjections often play an important part in this disturbance. He has identified with an idea or a situation, once and for all, and projects this belief onto the outside world. He lives all experiences through a filter which falsifies his perceptions and only partially allows for learning. The disturbances of the personality-function therefore alter his vision of the past, his perception of the present, and block his growth and plans.

Natalie has based her identity on a double introjection which disturbs her personality-function: "men are dangerous and I must do as well as they." She has exhausted herself in the quest for social success, avoids any emotional contact with the male world, and is vehemently not interested in considering having children.

• The disturbances of the **ego-function** are a consequence of the two previous disturbances: if the individual is wrong about his sensations and who he basically is, he has no chance of making good choices, of engaging in satisfactory actions. The contact-boundary between the organism and the environment is disturbed. In therapy we cannot therefore contribute to the fluidity of the function of the self, while the other two elements remain rigid. It is sometimes a source of frustration for a client who would like to know rapidly "what to do with my life..."

I remember Natalie's astonished look, during our last therapy session. With her eyes full of tears, she said to me: "I haven't yet found happiness, nor the man of my life, nor the child that I would like to

> *have, but I feel ready for them because I feel really* **me**, *and that's the first step toward peace...* "

Creative adjustment and awareness

The idea of creative adjustment rightly completes the notion of self. Creative adjustment is our way of adapting, in the best way possible, to personal needs and to an environment which is permanently changing.

The artisan of this adaptation to the world is the self. Developing one's creative adjustment is the very foundation of all Gestalt Therapy. Being able to adapt first supposes being able to feel what is happening in us: that's *awareness*, that is, realizing what our body is saying, what emotions we are going through.

> *In this permanent flux of sensations, of needs, of desires, of rejections, I select and allow to come to consciousness those which seem the most pertinent at a given moment. So I can suddenly realize, through a muscular feeling, that I need to rest. But I might also have filtered and ignored this feeling, taken up with the enthusiasm I feel for writing!*

To use a car metaphor, *awareness* is therefore made up of the totality of detectors and dials which make up the dashboard; they give constant information on the state of the engine, on the weather, on the right road to take. You still have to look at them and they still have to give correct information! And it's also important not to ignore one's feelings (*non-existent awareness*) or to make a mistake about what one is feeling (*disturbed awareness*).

Creative adjustment is the totality of decisions which the driver makes, taking the dials into account, but also everything that has not been foreseen: a threat of ice, an incident on the road, tiredness, or the meeting for which one must not be late!

Creative adjustment is therefore the possibility in a given situation of finding the best balance[62] between needs and environmental resources. Goodman emphasized this theme[63]: he distinguished, on the one hand, the *conservative* adjustments which concern physiology (to allow the organism to stay alive), and on the other hand, *creative* adjustments which we develop in a perspective of growth: "It is through contact that the organism grows. Creative adjustment is never disappointing."

The organism is therefore caught between two demands:
• The permanent maintenance which Goodman calls self-preservation, so that one does not dissolve into the environment;
• The need for an imbalance, an opening, a receptivity to the new so as to maintain a dynamic of evolution and growth.

Throughout his social and political involvement, Goodman remained true to this key idea: "It is only that which preserves itself that can grow through assimilation, and it is only that which assimilates the new which can preserve itself and not degenerate." [64]

Developing creativity, that is, the capacity to invent new forms, in the Gestalt sense of the word, is an important pole of therapy. The self, as a process of contact with the environment, favors the creation of new forms and figures. For this newness to find a space, one needs to destroy old structures and to favor assimilation, that is the function of aggressiveness.

---

[62] This is the principle of homeostasis.

[63] Chapters 12 and 13 of *Gestalt therapy, op. cit.*

[64] Chapters 12 and 13 of *Gestalt therapy, ibid*

Healthy aggressiveness

It was in his first book[65] that Perls developed this concept, which we regularly apply in Gestalt. It distinguishes between paranoid aggressiveness which is turned towards the destruction of an enemy, and *biological aggressiveness* which is indispensable to our survival (from *ad gressere* in Latin, which means "to go towards").

This validation of healthy aggressiveness is sometimes misunderstood. It should not be a justification for hatred, destruction, or war, but on the contrary, an involved encounter, a "full contact" between the environment and oneself.

Perls validated the "hunger instinct" with the well known metaphor of the apple; he explained that to feed ourselves, we must first cut and separate a piece with our incisors, then chew with our molars. These two operations are indispensable for a successful assimilation, that is, to avoid introjections. Perls distinguishes between total introjection (the baby who drinks milk) from partial introjection (biting) and assimilation (chewing). Our organism needs destruction to ensure growth; we need to be aggressive to make progress. Biological aggressiveness is a life force.

Therapy often requires work on the "regurgitation" of introjections, that is, what we have "swallowed whole" during our upbringing. We then need to "chew over again" what seems worthwhile, to integrate it into our personality, and reject what we no longer want.

> *Peter suffered from a very strict education. He was sent away to a religious boarding school at a very young age and was crushed by an austere atmosphere whose values he didn't understand. Many activities were forbidden, religious practices imposed, and his frustrations*

---

[65] *Ego, Hunger and Aggression, op. cit.*

increased with time. He came to therapy as a timid, introverted person, suffering from sudden phobias. He spent all his energy bandaging his childhood traumas.

In a group, following the work of one member about his failure at school, Peter discovered a sudden anger against those "sadists" who ruined his childhood. During several sessions, he could only express hostility, sometimes with spectacular emotion, against any form of restriction of youth. One day he dared to tear up a large piece of paper symbolizing one of his teachers and he reduced it to confetti which "flew" away. He swore at the confetti which continued to "dirty his carpet," and stick to him. He finally found his own solution, to go and find the vacuum cleaner in the cupboard and in a great explosion of laughter, to get rid of these bits of torn up paper.

He stopped suddenly, and decided to keep certain bits of paper, because he said, "in all that torment, I still had some good friends who taught me the meaning of solidarity."

It was by accepting the dimension of healthy aggressiveness that Peter developed his autonomy with regard to his upbringing, sorting out what suited him and what he wanted to get rid of. Some months later, he noted that "this rejection of his educational upbringing," as he put it, no longer affected what he discovered in therapy, that is, the pleasure of learning and exploring.

Polarities

Working on polarities seems to me to be one of the most "efficient" elements of Gestalt Therapy. The concept probably comes from Eastern philosophy. We saw, in part one, that Perls was very interested in Eastern philosophy, in particular under Paul Weisz's influence. The Tao speaks to us of yin and yang, of the feminine and the masculine, of shadow and light. We never have just one characteristic, one pathology, one way of being in the world. Exploring the "opposite," the shadowy zone which we don't know, or which we refuse to acknowledge is always a rich source of discovery.

The Gestalt concept of polarities, by suggesting that each of our personality traits has an opposite is more supple than Jung's theory which talks of the great archetypes. For example, it is by accepting his feminine polarity that a man is fully expressed as a man, or in cultivating his diabolical side that he finds his archangel…

In the protected laboratory which is the "psychotherapeutic office" for individuals or groups, the client can dare to explore feelings and attitudes that are unfamiliar to him.

> *Paul is a quiet and reserved young man. He is having difficulties in his relationship. He is hurt by the supposed infidelity of his partner, without daring to question her on the matter. So he seems anaesthetized, has become indifferent, and his sexuality, dormant.*
>
> *In an individual session, he dared to play "the spy" and exaggerated his jealousy, explored with delight the wastepaper basket in my office, pretending that he was searching his partner's pockets. In short, he dared to make gestures that he would feel were "sacrilegious" in his real life.*
>
> *After this time of "emotional discharging" when he enjoyed "raging," I gently brought him back to the concrete reality of his life as a couple. He decided to dare to evoke his doubts with his wife, to talk of his jealousy and the freedom they could give one another. It is the exploration of a taboo polarity in him, "spying," which has allowed him to make an adjustment between the need for affective security and the love he feels for his partner.*

Joseph Zinker[66] described the disturbed person as someone who lives in a unilateral and stereotypical way; that is, who is unable to navigate easily between opposing polarities. On the contrary, a healthy person can accept feeling contradictory feelings, complex emotions and develop creativity through adjustment.[67] This person could say, "In general, I am very gentle, but in an unfair situation, I like to be hard, which helps me to defend myself."

I would now like to develop this idea with an example which I witnessed in a company.

---

[66] Zinker J. *Se créer par la Gestalt*, Montreal, Editions de l'homme, 1981.

[67] Masquelier G., "Gestalt and pedagogy" in *La Gestalt et ses différents champs d'application*, Paris, Journées d'études SFG, 1985.

I was called in as a consultant for a team of car salesmen. After a morning of "ice breaking" and of mutual discovery, I suggested that they collectively name some characteristics of their style of work. They described themselves as brave (with extremely long work days), obstinate (never giving up on a potential sale) and competent (knowing their trade very well).

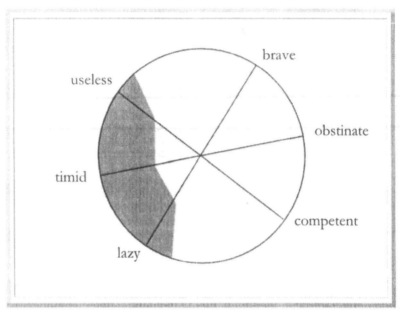

I wrote these three adjectives round the edge of a large circle on the paperboard and asked them to name their opposites. The opposite of brave became lazy, obstinate became timid, and competent became useless. I concentrated on the word lazy and suggested that we explore this new polarity in themselves.

After some hesitation, as if "sales people" could not imagine this "shadow area," they relaxed and I helped them to name advantages which might come with laziness. Then various words came out which mentioned their physical and emotional tiredness, the difficulties in their families due to their overlong working hours, their stress.

In short, I invited them to explore and accept the possibility of "sometimes being lazy" and to discover its potential advantages: "I'd be less tired, my back would hurt less, I'd sometimes come home earlier."

During this course, and with the agreement of the director, this team designated a daily "Mr. Lazy." The expression became fashionable. In turn, about once every two weeks, each sales rep was "forbidden to travel." He had to stay in the office, and use his time to catch up with his paperwork and organize himself. He was free to receive visitors, to give them a better reception, to get them a coffee and to answer all their questions without being stressed. In other words, "Mr. Lazy" is not useless, but is someone who, for one day, lives differently from the others.

This decision improved everyone's quality of life, the functioning of the team, the welcoming of clients. It was the acceptance of an attitude which had been *a priori* "banned" for salesmen, which in fact, stimulated their creativity.

Work on polarities therefore consists in discovering how to diminish our blind spots, that is, those that we refuse, those that we don't see or those that frighten us. Americans have an expression that I like to use, "*What's good about it?*" What is good in this situation, in this feeling, in this polarity, that we may be refusing?

To finish this commentary, I would like to emphasize an idea that I cherish, that the world is never bipolar. There are always multiple contradictions to a given idea or situation. So for example, during the course that I have just described, one participant chose as the opposite of "brave," the word "realist"; what he meant by that was that with the low salary that he received, working hard would be mere foolishness...

In couple's therapy, for example, the opposite of "happily married" is not necessarily "divorced." There can be multiple facets for a realigning of conjugal status.

Gestalt in a few lines...

The principle concepts of a Gestalt approach are more easily understood when one looks at them globally, in a dynamic[68] and historical perspective.

Perls started out with the idea of introjection: that we must chew things over again to allow assimilation. Then Goodman developed the concepts of the unity of the organism-environment (the field) and exchanges at the contact-boundary (the self). When tension is created at this boundary (resistance) and we notice it (awareness), then we search for a new balance (homeostasis). Ideally, we get there by a creative adjustment which allows for growth. Our different polarities favor this creative adjustment.

The specificity of Gestalt Therapy can be summed up, in my opinion, in these few lines. To be still more succinct, I would say that it has taken us from a traditional **intra**-psychic approach to an **inter-psychic** approach in which an organism cannot be separated from its environment.

---

[68] I evoked in the introduction, the fact that Gestalt takes us from a photographic to a cinematic view of the psyche.

Existential pressures

A ny therapy is based on philosophical reflection, that is to say a questioning of human nature, our evolution and our future. A philosophical approach is also an inquiry into good and evil, feelings, the meaning of life and spirituality.

Existentialism seems to me to be one of the most fertile sources for Gestalt Therapy and deserves our attention. It was Noel Salathé who best formalized what existential philosophy has brought to Gestalt Therapy: moreover he defines Gestalt as being "the therapeutic branch of existentialism."[69]

Anxiety

The Gestalt approach is based on two fundamental existentialist concepts: the proposition of freedom and responsibility.

The **proposition of freedom** is a central axis: man is not predestined, he recreates his existence every single day. Man is not determined completely by his unconscious, "his Oedipus complex" or his instinctual drives. Man searches every day for the conditions of his balance. So, therapy is the occasion to broaden his "range of possibilities," in order to develop a "creative adjustment." The objective is to re-establish the ability to choose.

---

[69] Salathé Noël, *Psychothérapie existentielle: une perspective gestaltiste,* Paris, Amers, 1989.

This proposition is beautifully illustrated by one of Sartre's thoughts: "The most important thing is not what has been done with me, but rather, what I do with what has been done with me."[70]

> *I think that it is in this proposition that my vocation as a therapist is based. Indeed, what is the point of my work if I am not convinced that my client has the potential to evolve, to free himself from his neuroses through a personal journey? What is the point of investing time or energy if the client is forever the victim of an old trauma?*
>
> *This book emphasizes the idea that nothing is ever taken for granted and that we are neither predestined, nor conditioned, nor permanently marked by our past. Life is offered to us, even imposed on us, but our existence is re-created every day. This may seem rather too optimistic, but I have often been able to verify the truth of this affirmation in both my professional and private lives.*

The corollary of this proposition of freedom, the "price to be paid," is the feeling of **responsibility**. To feel responsible for one's actions, to develop the ability to choose, can cause anxiety. *Angustus* in Latin means "tightened" (when I have tonsillitis, my throat is tightened). Anxiety is therefore both a physical and psychological manifestation. From childhood onwards, we become aware of the realities of human nature and this contributes to the forging of our personalities.

The tendency nowadays places the creation of anxiety earlier and earlier in the development of the child. Freud situates it at the Oedipal moment, that is to say between three and five years of age (castration anxiety). British psychoanalysts[71] propose as evidence the "anxiety of the eight-month old" (so-called "separation anxiety") when the baby differentiates itself from its mother and is afraid of losing her. Among them, Melanie Klein puts forward the

---

[70] Interview given to *L'Arc* in October 1966.

[71] Anna Freud, Rene Spitx, Donald Winnicott, Michael Balint, etc.

theory of an older anxiety, allied to the fear of destroying or being destroyed by the "good/bad breast."

Otto Rank, through his writing on the trauma of birth[72] and subsequently Frédéric Leboyer in his research into "childbirth without violence" both describe the anxiety of the newborn, expulsed from the uterus and projected into a difficult world. Jouvet, who works with dreams, believes that the mother communicates every night to her fetus the "great book of images" of what she has lived through during the day, but also her desires and anxiety, and that's how the inheritance of humanity is transmitted.[73] Anxiety may therefore envelope us *in utero*. And finally, Woody Allen "filmed" the anxiety of sperm: two hundred million competitors hurl themselves forward at the same moment and there is only one fortunate winner that penetrates the ovule.

Karen Horney, on the other hand, describes anxiety as being existential, that is to say written into the heart of humanity itself. Sexuality and aggressiveness would then be healthy responses to this basic existential anxiety. They would ensure the survival of the species.

Sexuality

Freud placed sexuality as the central axis of human development. We have already seen that Perls' first book is a critique of this theoretical position. We can understand sexuality to be *one* of the components of the human psyche, a fundamental idea, but *not the only one.*

Let us distinguish "genital pleasure" which designates the sexual act, from "sexuality," which is a much greater idea, involving both

---

[72] Rank O., *Le traumatisme de la naissance,* Paris, Payot, 1968.
[73] A pregnant woman doubles the average length of her dreams.

pleasure and incompleteness. Sexuality comes from the Greek word, *secare*, meaning "to cut or separate. "

In *The Banquet*,[74] Plato tells a beautiful story: in the past, human beings were "creatures with two backs" that is to say a man and a woman, or two men,[75] were linked together though their stomachs, with four legs, four arms, etc. They were perfectly happy. But curiosity made them want to visit the home of the gods who, to punish them, decided to split them in two. They thereby lost their other half and since that time, travel the world, moaning and groaning, trying to find "their other half."

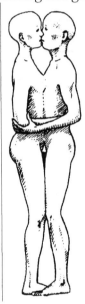

For the beauty of the image, I should add that, according to Plato, the belly button is the scar which was all that was left to man, at the moment of separation, like the two halves of an apple.

Sexuality is therefore this feeling of lack, of incompleteness. An individual cannot be complete on his own, neither for reproductive purposes, nor for access to complete happiness. Alone, he will never be able to know "the other half of the world."

He may try to negate this frustration and turn in on himself, hoping to be self-sufficient, but then he will find only solitude. He can multiply his sexual experiences in the hope that, one day, someone will fill his emptiness, his lack. Or, he can enter into fusion, by developing a kind of confluence. But these approaches are often destined to fail, or simply impose a great deal of renunciation. No one has a "perfect

---

[74] Plato, *The Banquet*, Paris, Flammarion.
[75] Plato thereby justifies male homosexuality… but forgets to mention lesbianism.

kindred spirit" who would fill all his emptiness, satisfy all his desires (even if Plato suggests the opposite—for him there was one person, and one person only who would fit completely with the other, like two pieces of a broken stick[76]).

Therapy must help the client to accept both the pleasure of joining with another as well as the frustration of incompleteness.

> *When a couple is expecting a baby, much attention is given to the future mother: advice, congratulations, social esteem, and that is just as it should be. My clinical and personal experience (I have four children) shows that men often go through a difficult stage: regret at not being able to go through the great adventure of maternity although this includes weight gain, anxiety, jealousy. One speaks of the tie of childbirth. If we could only change gender, for a day, a month, a year… Here we find again the theme of polarities.*

The five principal pressures

Noel Salathé spoke about "existential constraints," that is, unavoidable realities that we can't escape from and which generate in us a sort of anxiety, specific to the human destiny. Death, for example, is unavoidable and can generate fear, denial and depression, etc. Salathé has since changed his formula and now speaks of "fundamental existential ideas."

"Existential" comes from the Latin *sistere*, "to be placed," and from *ex*, "outside of." It is precisely because we have been "thrown into the world" as Heiddeger says, separated from our mothers, that we feel these anxieties.

Personally, I speak of existential pressures, that is, a source of energy, which can, of course, generate anxiety, but can also create enjoyment of life and enthusiasm. So it is partly because life is

---

[76] To understand this, it is enough to compare our belly buttons and to verify that they are identical.

short that I like to make the best of every day, so as not to waste it; the *Carpe Diem*[77] put forward by Virgil. Life is a search for balance: if I'm in too much of a hurry, I may be overwhelmed; but how sad it is to be depressed!

The five principal pressures developed by the existentialists are: finality, solitude, responsibility, imperfection and the search for meaning. I would like to examine each of these themes in turn and the psychological manifestations which they engender and how Gestalt Therapy can help us to find our own answers.

Finality

Very early in life, a child encounters the reality of finality, that is, death. All living beings, but also all activities and objects, come to an end. Understanding this can come at the moment of a death in the family, of the loss of a favorite pet, or the breaking of a toy, for example. But many other events put us under these existential pressures: divorce is the death of the couple, unemployment is the rupture of professional life, an argument can be the end of a friendship. What are our personal strategies in relation to this reality?

It seems to me that we have three principal choices:

• We can either speak of "constraint" and we hit a wall against which we will break, that's the path of depression: what's the point of starting a relationship if it must stop one day, what's the point of investing yourself in work if you risk losing it, what's the point of living if everything must come to an end one day...

• Or, we can seek to deny this constraint by forgetting death, by denying it and making it commonplace. Society today doesn't prepare children for this aspect of the human condition: older members of society and cemeteries are kept at a distance, and we die in a hospital. On the other hand, the saturation of violent

---

[77] "Seize the day."

images or of accidents in the media, makes these traumas seem commonplace: I am struck by the fact that children usually don't make any connection between the weapons they use for their war games and the images of the massacres they see on the television news.

• Or, we can speak of "existential pressures" and we can see our finality as a great appeal to life as the poet Ronsard invites us: *"Gather the roses of life today…"*

Many of our actions can be questioned as a response, our own personal response to this finality. Having children is one way of prolonging oneself through inheritors; building a house or planting a tree, writing a book – are they not all partial responses to this finality? Everyone has heard of the Egyptian pharaohs because they built the pyramids… Investing oneself completely in research, in a career, or a passion is another way of transmitting one's name to posterity.

> *My partner and I created a center for drug addicts, a farm in the countryside where we cared for young people who were in psychological trouble, for long periods. After five sometimes-difficult years, it seemed sensible to me to hand it over to others. I could only make that decision after publishing a book about our experience, as though writing was a way of saying "farewell" and not "goodbye."*[78] *It was as if, by leaving a trace which people still often talk to me about, I was able to keep a link with that part of my life which had contributed to my maturity.*

Gestalt, which some people call the *therapy of the here and now*, is right at the heart of this question. That is to say, what are we going to decide to do, here and now, with our past, with our future, which we know to be limited?

---

[78] Masquelier G., *Drogue ou liberté, un lieu pour choisir*, Paris, Editions Universitaires, 1983.

The idea of creative adjustment, for example, shows clearly that, by facing the unavoidable reality that is our finality, we can find multiple ways of positioning ourselves.

Solitude

The existential pressures of finality and solitude generally go together, they are related: we are alone with death, there comes a time when no one can accompany us in that ordeal. We can feel three types of solitude; depending on different periods of our lives and our personalities, one or another of them can become more painful.

• We feel *interpersonal* solitude, that is, the feeling of being cut off from others, of not having any friends. To mask this solitude, we can have lots of casual relationships, but the feeling of emptiness remains. It is also the frustrating feeling of never being able to communicate completely with other people. Modern life, which goes by so fast, exacerbates this feeling of solitude; we can feel alone in a crowd. Many people coming into therapy have this problem.

• Another sign is *intra-personal* solitude, that is, the feeling of being cut off from oneself. Not only can I not be in perfect harmony with others, but I realize that I can't even be in "real contact" with myself. I don't know what I want, I don't know who I am, I'm led by my unconscious self without knowing it. This is the "know yourself" beloved of the Greeks. For some people, depression begins as soon as they stop, take time to listen to their bodies or their hearts—and find that they are living with a stranger: themselves.

• Finally we are aware of a third form of solitude which we can call an *existential* solitude. Fundamentally we are alone in the world. Might there be a link between the universe and myself? Is there, as Voltaire asked, "a Great Watchmaker," a Creator, or are we here by chance, like the grains of sand on a beach? The word religion comes from the Latin *religare* which means "to link". Religion is a link between men who acknowledge themselves as being from the same Father or believers in the same faith.

These great existential questions are accentuated at certain times in life and are often amplified after a bereavement or trauma.

> *Jo came into group therapy with severe depression, on the advice of a psychiatrist. We explored "the father who didn't believe in him," "the mother who preferred his younger sister," "the classmates who made fun of him." I became desperate about Jo... we had more and more sessions, but nothing seemed to get through to him.*
>
> *Sometimes there was one ray of hope: when we talked about computers... I hung on to that light in his eyes: he was playing at being the center of the universe, "the mega-super-extra system" that rules the country; another day, he identified with his computer screen, cold and flat, but which can write everything, show everything, the moment a friend turned on the keyboard.*
>
> *A friend? What friend?*
>
> *At last, his heart opened. Jo had been living in terrifying solitude: he spent his time inventing computer programs alone at home, from morning to night. An excess of inter- and intra- personal solitude was hidden by his computer[79]; he was not aware of it, but depression was taking the upper hand...*
>
> *After becoming aware of all this, it took him more than a year, thanks, among other things, to the warmth and encouragement of the group, to switch his screen off at six p.m. and begin to redevelop friendships and a social life.*

---

[79] One day he made a slip and called the computer "enfermatique" instead of "informatique" (in French, *informatique* means *computer, enfer* means *hell*).

The Gestalt therapist pays attention to the contact-boundary. He is therefore particularly attentive to what is relevant regarding inter- and intra- personal solitude, as I was able to be with Jo. Fear of existential solitude is often deeply hidden and in general only emerges when the therapeutic alliance is strongly established.

Responsibility

This theme was especially developed by Sartre and Camus. Taking responsibility means recognizing that one is the undisputed actor of an event. The existential pressure of responsibility is the corollary, the consequence of our freedom. It is therefore beneficial, but also can be a source of anxiety because, for example, if one fails, one can't hide behind another person or an external cause. As early as 1947, in his first book, Perls insisted on the use of the first person singular and suggested, "I dropped the cup" instead of "the cup slipped out of my hands."

Our responsibility comes into play when we have freedom of choice, when desire is awakened. The process happens in three stages: first, we have a desire or a need; then, we have the freedom to say yes or no; and finally, we choose to put it into action or not. We have multiple strategies to side-step this fundamental existential idea:

• We can extinguish our desire, so as not to have to confront the difficulty of decision making: "to choose is to die a little," as a popular saying goes.

• We can relinquish our freedom, by giving it to others. The current phenomenon of religious sects can be seen in this light; it is easier when we are told what to do, when we are told right from wrong, so as to avoid distressing questions. Gestalt, with its emphasis on responsibility, is opposed to any drifting into sects.

• Finally, we can avoid putting our desires into action, by choosing the path of immobility, thereby avoiding the risk of failure; but this may sometimes lead to depression...

Responsibility often generates guilt: for example, an individual may feel guilty at not succeeding more in relationships, at not bringing up his children as he had dreamed, etc. This guilt can be well-founded (the person is truly responsible for such a failure) or neurotic (the person feels guilty for failures for which he is not really responsible – which accounts for so much of the sadness in the world!).

> *Marie was constantly angry with her husband. That's what had brought her into therapy. I've written "what brought her" because she couldn't even take responsibility for her choice: "I'm here because he is horrible." It was impossible to start any therapeutic work while this defense mechanism was active. It took several individual sessions for Marie to be able to admit: "I'm here because I need to be; I'm taking the risk that my relationship may change by this action of mine."*

In therapy, we can focus on the idea of guilt or on the three steps of the process,[80] which gives us several ways of intervening within Gestalt.

• If guilt is the dominating force, the therapist searches for what needs to be activated to "repair" the things that have been done.

> *Marie feels responsible for the death of a child in a car accident that she caused. Her involvement in an association for the protection of children is, in part, a response to this tragedy.*

---

[80] Eliminating my desire, giving up my freedom, or avoiding putting my desire into practice.

• The therapist can center himself on the desire and look for a way of reactivating it. This can be done through body work: "What am I feeling? What is my body telling me right now? What is my breathing doing? " These are all questions that may be very helpful.

• The therapist can reactivate the ability to choose. The choice of saying "I," rather than "we" or "one," can help the client to situate himself, to become aware of his needs.

• The therapist can work on "acting out." In a situation which is blocked, he can explore how to help the client move from "I can't" to "I don't want to," and by simply changing the verb in the sentence, reintroduce responsibility. Then one can imagine removing the negative, to dare to say, "I want to" and then, finally making the decisive declaration: "I will."

I used this approach a lot with Marie. Her position, as regards the possibility of change in her relationship was even more defensive: "I can't because he doesn't want to." Finding access to her own desire took a long time. We used drawing ("what would be your ideal house?") and mime ("let's act out Marie the vamp, Marie the perfect mother, Marie who is a success") before discovering which, of all these ideas, were attainable.

The search for a therapeutic I-Thou relationship is an excellent way of highlighting the existential pressure of responsibility. But if the anxiety is too strong, the Gestalt therapist may introduce "a shuttle" between an I-It position, in which he assumes a greater directivity in the unfolding of the process, to return as soon as possible to the I-Thou relationship, which involves more sharing of responsibility.

Imperfection

This existential tension is related to the preceding one of responsibility. Each human being is responsible for his actions because he is free: therefore he suffers from the delay between his desires and their fulfilment, between the image he has of himself and the image of himself which he receives back from his daily life. In short, he is a limited being.

For example, as in the image of the glass that is half-empty or half-full, depending on the optimism or the pessimism of the moment, he may feel the existential restriction of the imperfection which blocks him, and this may cause him to despair. Or rather, an incentive towards perfection, which may stimulate him and motivate him to search, study or improve his actions and relationships.

To escape this limitation there are many different strategies:

• One strategy is to become a megalomaniac, to have the feeling of belonging to a superior race and of being misunderstood by others.

• Another strategy is not to try anything for fear of failure, going instead into a dream world where everything is possible.

• Some people, and this is the most often used strategy, look for a scapegoat, that is, finding someone else who is responsible for one's own difficulties and limitations. Finding that scapegoat gives them an excuse for their imperfections, that is, it deflects their anxiety. The scapegoat is in this case a deflection of their own feelings of guilt and anxiety.

Yet again, history demonstrates this idea of deflection of anxiety. The ancient Greek cities kept a prisoner who had been captured in war, and allowed him to live in great luxury. He had the same rights and benefits as the other citizens: he could make fun of anyone, seduce women, wear the most beautiful clothes and eat the best food. However, he couldn't leave the town. If any source of anxiety appeared, such as, war, famine or epidemic, then this prisoner who was called the *pharmakos*, was taken outside the city walls and stoned to death in hopes of deflecting the danger. In this way the people could exorcise their fear and reinforce their cohesion. *Pharmakos* became... the pharmacist, that is, the person who "has what it takes" to cure us.

> *So Marie accused her husband of being responsible for the difficulties in their relationship: when the "scapegoat" wasn't her husband, it would be her husband's boss who stressed him and made him work late. During therapy Marie was able, on the one hand, to take responsibility for her relationship, and on the other hand, to tolerate the imperfections of both partners, that is, to accept the imperfections that come with any human relationship.*

In Gestalt Therapy, we try to reactivate the individual in relation to his fundamental choices: "What do you really need? What are you going to decide to do to get there?" The therapist must both help his client to recognize his boundaries when they seem reasonable, and yet encourage him to push beyond them, when they are limited or sterile.

The search for meaning

Depending on our view of the world, we can call this existential pressure, "the search for meaning," with all the energy that comes out of that, or else, "the absurdity of existence," with a nihilistic perspective. The search for meaning covers two different questions which are however similar: "What is the meaning of my life?" and "What is the meaning of Life itself?" Each one of us is more or less aware of one or another of these existential questions.

The crisis in values in our society today as well as the breakdown of the family structure, make this search for meaning difficult. Many of my clients come into therapy with this questioning attitude. This search seems to me to be the synthesis of the four preceding ones: finality, solitude, responsibility and imperfection force each one of us to question the meaning of his or her own life as well as the meaning of Life in general.

There are many ways to avoid or engage the search for meaning; some are not satisfying in the long term...

• We can become workalcoholics, to avoid asking any questions at all.

• We can belong to a cult, a tradition, a religious sect. This is the zone of "you must," "it's always been done like that," and other conformist behaviors.

• We can become fanatics—fanaticism allows you to delegate your thinking to a superior authority: "All I have to do is do what I'm told!"

• We can become creative. Creativity, in all its forms (artistic, professional, social, familial) also allows us to give meaning to life.

All forms of therapy invite a search for meaning. Perls liked to question all dogmas and certainties. He would probably invite you to ask yourself the fundamental question first: "What is the meaning of **my** life?" When the answer to this question begins to be clear, then the second question appears, "What is the meaning of Life **itself?**"

Everyone is looking for answers, through philosophy, spirituality, social commitment, relationships, etc.

A life-giving fountain

This description of the five basic fundamental existentialist ideas could paralyze us. What's the point of living under these conditions? Nonetheless, our work in therapy shows us every day how these "limitations" can stimulate our creativity.

I'd like to finish this chapter with a metaphor... I see the psyche of each individual as being like a village fountain: five pipes channel the water from the ground—they are called finality, solitude, responsibility, imperfection and the search for meaning. The water comes up through a middle column and gushes out through different spouts—these are the aspects of the personality.

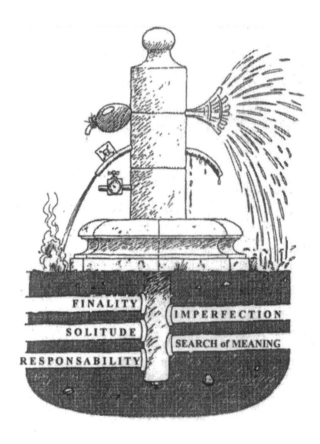

- When a person shows "sadistic" tendencies, the water gushes out in a boiling jet that showers upon passers-by;
- When a person is "histrionic" the water comes out in the form of soap bubbles in glistening colors, so that everyone can admire them;
- When a person has "paranoid traits" they poison the water, because a passer-by might attack them;
- When a person is "obsessive," they install a water-meter to measure consumption in liters, francs and Euro's;
- During "autistic" phases, one doesn't know how to unblock the spout which then swells up like a balloon;
- If the person feels "depressed" it means that the flow of water has stopped, or that there is a leak somewhere.

And finally, and this is what I wish for all of us, why not just let all the spouts gush out at once, because after all, water is **Life**...

The Gestalt intervention

G estalt is probably the current of therapy which puts the least emphasis on a particular technique, an analysis grille or a protocol of work. It may seem paradoxical to write that because one often quotes certain spectacular techniques, for example those that Perls particularly liked in his Californian period, which one often finds in the media, because they are easier to explain in a journalistic context. But an art form is not a collection of techniques.

I would like to emphasize that Gestalt Therapy is principally a way of being, centered on process and any concentration on techniques would deprive it of its originality.

Having taken this precaution, let's study some experimentation which can be seen in Gestalt work.

Monodrama

Monodrama consists of having a client play out one or several of the actors concerned by the problem he is working on.

> *Mark is angry with his wife, because she spends too much money. This is a recurrent difficulty in their marriage, but the problem has become worse since Carol has been unemployed: she is no longer contributing to the family budget... and she has more time for shopping.*
> *He expresses very rationally all the arguments about the importance of "putting money to one side," and explores several feelings of insecurity*

and misogyny, but nothing seems to "make sense," that is, to give meaning to what he feels.

So I suggest that he "act as" Carol and try to experience some new feelings. After several minutes, he takes a ream of paper, pretends each page is a 500 Euro bill, and begins to throw all these bills around with growing pleasure: soon there are bills all around the room. Mark rolls around these bills with pleasure.

Suddenly a breeze carried one of the bills out of the open window: this was a revelation to Mark. He stopped, looked at me with shining eyes, and finally found a meaning to his jealousy of Carol: "She at least, is free: I envy her carefree attitude — I'd love to be less anxious in life."

The real signification for Mark was therefore not money, but freedom. By stimulating our imagination, by mobilizing our body and our emotions, the monodrama often allows us to explore a hidden face of our problem. Spontaneity and games break down our defenses, or at least allow us to go around them. Here we are talking about a real "incarnation" of the word.

The goal is not to imitate, or be credible, but rather, to slide into the skin of another person, to look at the same reality with different eyes. This work is particularly interesting when there is a conflict, for example in a couple or with children. In fact, the monodrama allows one to play one character, with several facets to his personality, but also to become someone else, or to shed light on a feeling, a fear, etc.

We find in this technique Perls' passion for the theatre and stage production. We use the term monodrama when the client is "alone on stage." When in a group, he may choose one or several partners, which may allow him to see his own character as played by another participant; in this case, we use the term *psychodrama*, according to the term used by Moreno.[81]

Enactment

Gestalt is a holistic psychotherapy (from the Greek *holos*, "whole"), that is, it seeks to work with the whole individual, without separating the body from thoughts, emotions, etc. It is therefore a contradiction to say that Gestalt Therapy does "body work," as though the head or heart of the client were forgotten.

This choice of a holistic mobilization during therapy presupposes that a client can respect the difference between *acting out* and *enactment*.

• *Acting out* is an avoidance,[82] often impulsive and defensive, which doesn't allow for a new awareness. The therapeutic framework which defines the working conditions in Gestalt, supposes a prohibition of any acting out, in particular anything violent or sexual.

• *Enactment* is a bodily and emotional mobilization which favors awareness. It allows the exploration of unknown or repressed feelings. As I specified in chapter three, this sort of work involves three phases: an approach to the difficulty, an enactment and a time of elaboration. The last stage is indispensable for the client to be able to integrate what he has just discovered, but this stage can be postponed if the emotional charge of the second stage was strong.

> *A typical example is that of the "territorial defense:" Mark received a*
> *very strict education which taught him to suppress any need for*

---

[81] Jacob Levy Moreno was the creator of psychodrama, group psychotherapy based on theatrical games, and was the author of *Group psychotherapy and psychodrama,* Paris, Retz, 1975.

[82] Ginger S. and A., *Gestalt, a Therapy of Contact, op.cit.*

independence or freedom, because such a need would be socially maladjusted. I suggested an enactment of this need: he created a territory around himself with a few cushions placed on the carpet, and the other group participants tried to invade his domain. By looking for gestures to affirm his need for autonomy without attacking others or hurting himself, Mark was able to explore new ways of behavior and tried to find the best place for each person. He then experienced a creative adjustment, between the necessity for rules in society and his own autonomy, which guarantees its vitality.

For this enactment to be useful, it's indispensable that it should be created in the here and now between the therapist and the client. I mean by this that it must never be decided in advance, that enactment must not be an obligatory passage through which every client must pass during his therapy. I emphasize this idea because a group naturally has a tendency to give itself "rules of good behavior," for example, to consider that the more spectacular the work is, the better it is. The therapist needs to remind the group that what is right for one is not necessarily right for the others.

One problem nevertheless remains difficult to resolve: at what moment should an action be considered *acting out?* Depending on the technique used, depending on the framework established, depending on the style of the therapist, depending on the quality of the therapeutic alliance, certain actions can either be regarded as *acting out* or not.

When Harnick, Perls' Berlin psychoanalyst, forbade him to marry Laura (after four years of living together) under threat of interrupting the analysis, he took a position of forbidding action and Fritz "acted out."

A Gestalt therapist would probably not have taken this rigid position: relying on the idea of responsibility, he would, I imagine, have helped his client to specify his need in relation to Laura's pressing request.

Amplification

Amplification is an intervention which is often used in Gestalt practice, and we use it in two ways:

The amplification of a gesture:

This is generally a tiny "micro-gesture" which the client often hasn't noticed:

Edward talks to me about his wife with a broad smile; she may sometimes be very annoying, but she is so fragile, so sweet that Edward "officially" feels only tenderness for her.

However his right thumb mashes his left palm. Copying his broad smile, I ask him to become this thumb and to amplify his mashing action.

After a few moments of surprise, Edward gets his right thumb to talk and discovers in himself a "monstrous desire" in his own words, to attack his partner. It will take him several sessions to admit that his love life is formed of contradictory feelings and that his body sometimes speaks on his behalf.

I look at Edward's gestures as bodily messages. I am sensitive to muscular contractions, to eyes that look away, to trembling, to blushing, to a voice that changes in intonation. I am also conscious of my own

micro-gesture: they give me information about what is going on in the I/Thou relationship. Sometimes I exaggerate them to show the client what his work is bringing up in me.

The amplification of a feeling:

This "bringing into the light" of a feeling is always a key time in therapy. We sometimes have emotions[83] which our upbringing has taught us to repress ("boys don't cry") or which we have associated with a traumatic memory. We have studied the interest of healthy aggressiveness to fight against these introjections and to develop creative adjustment.

Bodily mobilization, for example, shouting or making wild gestures, allows one to amplify an emotion, for example, anger, and to associate this emotion with a repressed memory which "comes back up to the surface." It's not important to know the "why" of this emotion, that is, the exact memory of what happened; it's more useful to feel the "how" it expresses itself today, in terms of bodily blockages, for example. We then talk about the cathartic effect.[84]

This emotional amplification is only useful if it is linked to a therapeutic process that heightens the client's awareness. To take up the metaphor of the river again, this amplification allows the client to develop new ways of allowing life to flow through him, in short to discover new figures of contact between himself and the environment.

---

[83] *motio* in Latin is a shiver (of fever) or a worry. *Movere* means "to put into movement."

[84] From the Greek *katharsis*, « purification. » For Hippocrates, good health requires the "disgorgement of overabundant humours."

Fundamental emotions:

These are: joy, surprise, fear, anger, sadness, disgust and contempt.[85] A composition of these different feelings gives a multitude of variants.

Sometimes, we don't have the words to speak of these emotions. They appear in all human cultures, with universal and innate facial expressions, as we know since Darwin's work in 1872.[86] This consistency of bodily expression of emotions is precious to me when I receive a client from a very different culture from my own, or when clients take up their mother tongue during regression work: without understanding the words, I can continue to accompany them through their non-verbal language.

These emotions can be associated to pre-verbal memories, that is, those that are hidden in our memory before we acquire language: fear of being abandoned, rejection of food, fear of suffocation during a difficult birth, etc. Bodily and emotional amplification then give us access to these traumas. Nevertheless, experience has shown me that it is important to put words onto the discharging of these emotions, sometimes many weeks later, so that they take on meaning during the course of a therapeutic treatment.

---

[85] Ekman P., *Emotion in the Human Face,* New York, Cambridge University Press, 1982.

[86] Darwin C., *The expression of the Emotions in Man and Animals,* Chicago, University of Chicago Press, 1965.

Emotional work

There are three main groups of emotional work:

• sequences of **discharging**, during which the client sometimes allows a very spectacular emotion to emerge: anger and fear are often present;

• sequences of **reparation**, when the client needs to "heal his wounds"; words, tears, the warmth of the group and the therapist allow him to go through this phase. Sadness is then the most frequent emotion;

• sequences of **experimentation**, during which the person dares to explore an unusual feeling or emotion. Therapy can be seen as a laboratory in which security, brought by the therapist and the professional milieu, permits the magnification of emotions, acts, and drives which would be unacceptable in the outside world.

The whole emotional register can then be gone through like a piano keyboard being played from pianissimo to fortissimo.

Speaking directly

Behind this expression is a hidden therapeutic lever which may seem insignificant at first, but which rapidly reveals its relevance. To understand it well, one needs to have experienced for oneself the profound difference between "talking **about** someone or something" and "talking **to** someone or something."

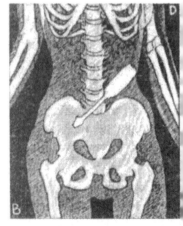

> *Sophie regularly talks to me about her stomach ulcer. That's why she has come to consult me. But the therapy is not progressing:*

> *she always puts the symptom forward, like a shield which prevents her from entering into contact with me or her emotions. She uses it to get sympathy, to find excuses for her depression, in other words to justify her immobility. One day I asked her to bring in an object which might represent her ulcer.*
>
> *The following week she arrived... with a screwdriver. Thanks to this object she's able to "talk **to** her illness," to "look at it straight on," to talk about her suffering but also her complicity: "I hate you, but sometimes you are useful..."*
>
> *This consciousness raising made her smile, and she decided not only to get well, but to also reorganize her life to make it more satisfying.*

Some months later, she left both her job and her ulcer! In speaking of her screwdriver, Sophie allowed a new figure to emerge: that of her relationship with her illness.

Yet again, the symptom is not so important in itself. My therapist's gaze was concentrated on "how she avoided full contact" in her life, and especially, during a session. It is the re-establishment of the capacity of exchange at the contact-boundary which allows for progress.

Perls advocates speaking directly to avoid two types of "chatter"[87] which he defined by the following neologisms:

• *aboutism*—in which we "talk about him and nothing happens"[88]
• *shouldism*—which he qualified as *moralism:* "hundreds of thousands of orders, but no consideration given to the person himself."

---

[87] In *Rêves et existence en Gestalt-therapie,* p19, *op.cit.*
[88] This has sometimes been called "*aproposisme.*"

Metaphor

In the preceding clinical example, I spoke about both direct questioning but also metaphor[89] which is a distancing technique which I use a lot. Metaphor is an analogy, that is, a symbolic expression, which is a helpful completion to verbal and body language. It means finding an object, choosing an image, making a drawing or a sculpture which distances the problem in order to be able to address it head on.

> *Jackie brings up a problem with her son: I suggest that she choose an animal to represent herself and another for her child. "With him, I feel like a songbird that has to bring up an elephant." The humor of the direct questioning between a songbird and an elephant, the creativity and the distancing technique, allow her to discover a hidden sense to her difficulties ("he's as heavy as my father was") and a new way of being ("...and what if I were to sing to him?")*

After this playful episode, it is indispensable to create a link between the metaphorical situation and reality. The choice of a metaphor generally reveals several meanings, symbolically condensed into one element.

> *It is for the client to determine the multiple meanings: being a songbird could be a plus (I'm free) or a minus (I'm like a butterfly that doesn't take responsibility for my role as a mother) or a sign of depression (I'm unable to fly).*

---

[89] From the Greek *meta* "change", and "*pherien* "to carry.

On the theoretical level, the Gestalt therapist therefore distinguishes himself from the traditions in which the therapist himself proposes his interpretation of the symbolic level.

Dream work

The book *Gestalt Therapy Verbatim* and the film that accompanies it present seminars on the theme of dream-work and have greatly contributed to the celebrity of its author. Perls insisted on the idea that each fragment of a dream can be considered as a part of the self. Integrating these different elements allows one to become a healthy, that is to say, unified person. According to him, dream images are not, as Freud suggested, the expression of a repressed desire, but rather the expression of creativity which is a trampoline from which we can better approach our current life.

> *Fritz recounted: " A patient dreamed that he left my office and went to Central Park. He crossed a path which riders used. So I asked him to "play the rider's path." He answered indignantly: "What? And let everyone walk all over me! — You see, he really felt the identification."*[90]

The Gestalt therapist therefore invites his client to play out several elements of the dream, considering that they are existential representations of his current life. It is often judicious to develop an unusual or minor element of the dream, like the riders' path, in order to stimulate the imagination and to discover the hidden potential of this dream production.

The enactment of the dream takes place in the "here and now," that is, the client will be encouraged to speak of it in the present tense: he doesn't recount his dream; but rather, he dives back into it, which allows him to possibly change it, to reclaim responsibility for the sequence of the scenes or for the way they ended. The dream is then regarded as "unfinished business" which must be reworked. Direct questioning, monodrama and amplification are often used. When working in a group, the different elements of the dream can be acted out by the participants as a psychodrama.

This identification work often has a double objective:
• that of allowing the integration of conflicts between the parts of the self represented in the dream;
• the acceptance of elements of ourselves which we consider to be negative and which we project onto the outside.

Finally the person who can't remember his dreams can challenge them directly, "Why are you running away from me?"

---

[90] In *Rêves et existence en Gestalt- thérapie* (1969), *op. cit.*

The use of transference

Transference is a psychological process in which the client reproduces, with the help of his therapist, attitudes or feelings which he felt in childhood. The use of transference in Gestalt Therapy is specific, that is, the therapist should not allow it to happen in a massive way; he tries to unknot it as they go along, so that the client can become aware of what he is setting up. Transference is a disturbance of the contact-boundary since the therapist is no longer encountered as he is in reality, but through the image that the client projects onto him.

This modification of the relationship is amplified in several ways:

• **emotional transference**, that is, the client relives the emotional situations of his childhood, whether good or bad;

• **support transference**, through which the client looks for the protection which he had or otherwise lacked in his life;

• **identification transference**, which incites the client to resemble his therapist, seen as stronger or happier.

These images can be named, enacted or amplified by role play and often imply quite a bit of emotional involvement.

> *Paul was in his sixties when he began individual psychotherapy. He suffered from depression which appeared at the beginning of his retirement: no work, a wife with whom he had lost the habit of communicating, three children who had left home; it is the well-known "empty nest" syndrome.*

> *For the first few months, he regressed and established a state of emotional dependency towards me, with "no taste for anything," in his own words. He seemed to expect everything from me: joie de vivre and solutions to his unhappiness. I tried without success to get him to explore different existential pressures such as finality and solitude, searching for a spark of energy or creativity.*

Then I suggested that he draw our relationship metaphorically and I do the same. After about ten minutes we compared our drawings. He drew me as a beautiful yellow car: he drew himself as an old, patched teddy bear on the back seat.

I drew myself as a fish who has met a starfish and is trying to persuade it to leave its rock...

After a few moments of surprise and laughter, the figure of our relationship gently emerged. He said "I feel old now, like this teddy bear, I'd like you to look after me—you could be my son and look after your old Dad, like I did for mine."

I understood, through my own drawing, that I refused to see him as exhausted, but that I was trying to persuade him to leave his rock and visit the ocean. Despite our difference in age, I saw him as a child whom I could encourage to greater autonomy.

Our contact boundaries are weighed down with transference images, or projections on one another; it is by elucidating them, as during this session, that a new creative adjustment takes place. By mobilizing our two "I's," a "We" was able to emerge.

In this example, I have evoked Paul's transference onto his therapist, but also my **counter-transference**. Counter-transference is the totality of psychological elements, sometimes conscious, but mostly unconscious, induced **in the therapist** by his client's personality.

This totality is composed of:

• the therapist's reaction to his client's transference: the therapist is not indifferent to the client's positive or negative feelings toward him;

• the therapist's own emotional history, in particular during his childhood, which generates an expression of transference by the therapist towards the client.

> *In practice, these two elements of counter-transference are intimately linked. I had a tendency to be constrained by the role of protective son which Paul gave me, while looking to stimulate his independence as my father did for me. The clarification of this double interference allowed Paul to take up his therapeutic path once more.*

One characteristic of transference and counter-transference is that there is always a "hidden person" in the relationship, that is, the presence of a third person. Paul wanted me to act as he did for his own father, for example. This paternal figure is present in the contact-boundary.

But it would be an over-simplification to think that all relationships are a summary repetition of the relationships we had with our parents. The emotions that arise between two people are also anchored in reality, and they express the authenticity of the encounter between two adults in the present moment.

To help clarify transference and counter transference, Perls proposed the attitude of *sympathy*,[91] that is, a "controlled

---

[91] From the Greek *sun* "with" and *pathos* "suffering."

involvement" on the part of the therapist, who draws from his own life to understand and accompany his client. He distinguished *sympathy* from the *empathy* recommended by Carl Rogers (which requires an unconditional acceptance of the other in order to be able to identify with him and feel his suffering), and from the psychoanalytical position, which Perls named *apathy* (a neutral attitude when facing the *pathos* of the client).

The challenge of the Gestalt position is to be able to be **both** fully involved in the relationship and, at the same time, to keep the necessary therapeutic distance; to be fully present in the contact with the client, while still keeping enough of a distance to be able to ask, "What is happening here, between us?"

In summary, what is exchanged at the contact-boundary is at the same time a real relationship as well as the reproduction of the client's previous situation (transference) and the therapist's previous situation (counter-transference).

THREE

CONTEMPORARY GESTALT

Fields of therapeutic application

Psychotherapy or personal development?

This question often comes up in new clients' questions. It's a recurring question, probably because there is no straight answer. There is no clear separation between the two approaches, but rather, a continuum which puts us more on one side, more on the other, depending on the frame of reference.

I am leading a three day seminar entitled "Gestalt and video." This seminar is centered on an emotional approach to "AutoShape," that is, that each person is invited to communicate directly with his own images on screen: to discover them, to experience them as multiple signs of his way of being in the world.

A ten-yard cable links the television and the camera, which allows a great deal of mobility. John is in the center of the group. For his first contact with Gestalt, he has chosen video because he can't bear to feel observed: as a primary school teacher in a small village, he feels permanently under observation, almost persecuted by his students, the parents and the mayor.

On the morning of the second day, he asks to work. First I film some images of him with the group and invite his reactions, to share what he feels: he names his muscular tension, his tightened breathing and invites me to come closer. Prudently, because I don't think I yet have his trust, I go behind him to show him an unusual view: "That's exactly how my students see me when I'm writing on the blackboard. That's when they could be throwing paper darts at me!"

Gradually his feelings become stronger and some micro-signs (his jaw and his hands relax) indicate that we have gotten to know one another, and that I am now going to be able to come nearer to him without a feeling of intrusion. I stand in front of him and do a close-up shot of his face.

He watches himself with emotion, "My dear little John, you look so scared!" I turn the lights down and change the focus on the camera to make it less sharp: only his dark eyes now come out of the gray of the screen.

"But those are my mother's eyes! They're always there judging me..." I invite to talk **to** *his mother, rather than talking* **about** *her: "Go away, I don't want to see you any more. I don't want to be judged."*

During this first seminar, is John in psychotherapy or personal development? It seems to me that there are three principal differences in these two terms:

According to **need**:
• In personal development, the need is targeted: "I've come to see you because I'm having problems with my relationship," or "I want to develop my creativity," or even, as for John, "I don't want to be scared of people looking at me any more."
Personal development is therefore close to the solving of problems or the self actualization of resources. The goal of feeling better about oneself is more present.
• In therapy, the need is often more open, more generic: "I've come because I'm suffering..." It's often linked to uncomfortable feelings about oneself, which can't be summed up in a few themes, an existential anxiety which has perhaps been awoken during a difficult chapter in life (mourning, children leaving home, unemployment).

Concerning the **duration**:
• Personal development can take place over several months, in occasional seminars or individual sessions.

In this way John had first signed up for a three-day seminar in Paris.

A deeper therapy is a real exploration of one's psyche, with its zones of light and its zones of shadows. It must necessarily be a long-term approach, perhaps taking several years.

At the level of **resistance**:
• The client in personal development comes with a more explicit request for progress. He therefore works principally on the defense mechanisms which are directly linked to the visible symptom. John, for example, became aware of an introjection: the hardness of his mother's gaze, a gaze that he projects onto others by thinking himself continually observed and judged.
• Each person, during therapy, is invited to explore his different resistances, to verify if they are still useful or if they are only the fossilized remains of the past.

Often the initial request is one of "personal development." Then, during the first months of work, some clients broaden their request and progressively enter the therapeutic path.

> *One month later, John telephoned me. His daily life as a primary school teacher has improved, but not his relationship with his mother. He wants to start individual therapy. I was surprised since I had not felt any such need at the end of the course. John spent two years in individual therapy. The major axis of the work was centered on his mother. The transference onto me was huge; depending on the moment, I had to be a welcoming mother or a frustrating one, an admiring one or a loving one.[92] The fore-contact period lasted about three months and the moment of engagement was made clear the day he decided to no longer wear a bracelet his mother had given him as a present. "I'm an adult, I want to dress myself and live my own life: and anyway, you are not my mother!"*

The treatment then evolved from an initial I-It relationship, where the symptom was important, to an I-Thou relationship, as the "therapeutic alliance" became established. It was then important to make a first summary: to visualize the path already taken, to readjust the initial demand, in short to make sense of this evolution. Like a well-constructed text, therapy needs punctuation marks which give it a rhythm and allow it to breathe.[93]

Let us now move on to the different modes of work proposed in France. To simplify my proposition, I will use the generic term "therapy" to designate any form of work on the self (thus leaving aside the expression "personal development").

---

[92] I could quote all the "ing" adjectives in the dictionary!

[93] Masquelier Chantal, « Ponctuation du travail thérapeutique » in *Revue Gestalt*, number 2, autumn 1991, pages 111-124.

Individual therapy

It is quite common, in France today, to begin with individual therapy. This is an approach that comes from both the medical and psychoanalytic models. It can seem easier to go and talk about one's problems in the intimate space of the consulting room.

The choice of a therapist is most often by word of mouth. The different training institutes and professional organizations distribute lists of qualified members.[94] It is quite normal to go and consult three or four therapists before making a decision.[95]

The first session or sessions allow contact to be made and the framework of treatment to be defined: the fees, the question of missed sessions, the question of confidentiality and professional ethics.

Individual therapy mostly takes place in weekly sessions of forty-five minutes to an hour. Sometimes, the therapist will suggest two sessions a week "for in-depth work" or during difficult times. A client base, for a therapist working full-time with individuals, is about thirty people.

The Gestalt therapist often offers a warm welcome. He does not hide behind an intimidating silence, but on the contrary, becomes involved, sometimes suggesting an experiment, highlighting an inconsistency, a gesture, something about the person's breathing. Depending on his personality and style, he may suggest a creative support, such as drawing or body work.

Some therapists work with couples: either both partners together, or alternative sessions with the couple followed by individual sessions for each partner.

---

[94] Thus at the Parisian Gestalt School, we get about five requests a day – which we pass on to our colleagues throughout France and even abroad.

[95] However it is sometimes the case that people consult a dozen therapists in the vain hope of getting free therapy!

Finally, a combination of group sessions and individual sessions is often a helpful formula: for example, one individual session a week and a monthly group session.

> *After working with John for two years, I have the feeling that the therapy is beginning to stagnate. I bring up my doubts in a supervision session and realize that we are probably coming to the end of a phase. John has explored all the facets of his relationship with his mother...*
>
> *He has given me "a maternal image" and doesn't want to consider me as a sexual being nor think that the "ideal mother" that I am for him might have several children of his own, that is, that I might have other clients as well. Unknotting the transference, making sense of the relationship that he has established with me, doesn't seem to be enough: "chase the transference away, it will come galloping back!"*
>
> *The relationship of fusion with his mother, who is the object of both love and hate, would probably evolve more easily in a group. I suggest this to him and he takes several months, in his own words, "to resign myself to it..."*

Naming the resistances without attacking them head-on, and taking the time to allow a new form to emerge, are necessary to the therapeutic process: that is what allows John to turn towards group work.

Group therapy

The majority of Europeans don't spontaneously think of this formula. In other countries, such as Mexico, which I know from spending six months there, it's traditional to practice Gestalt in groups: one only chooses individual therapy for reasons of isolation, if there are not enough people to create a group, or to finish a treatment.

Groups[96] are generally limited to a dozen people. They are sometimes co-led by a man and a woman, and if that is the case, can accept up to twenty participants, alternating between large and small groups. The advantage of being able to choose a male or female therapist,[97] to tackle certain subjects like sexuality or the relationship with parents, is obvious.

How does a group work? We often begin with some fore-contact time in which everyone talks about their lives, generally in a creative way, to favor personal involvement. Then there are times where individual participants "ask to work" that is, "dive" into their difficulties with the support of the therapist. The rest of the group serves as a mirror, an amplification of the situation which has been brought up, and also may share or reflect some of the emotions. At other moments, the whole group gets involved in a single theme which has emerged during the day.

There are three main categories of Gestalt courses with a therapeutic aim: occasional groups, ongoing groups and courses with a theme.

• **Occasional courses**

These last about three to five days and allow a discovery of the Gestalt process or the style of a practitioner: one can also find old clients who want, for the duration of a course, to see where they are now, or to recharge.

• **Thematic courses**

These allow the establishing of connections between different disciplines; *Gestalt and the Theatre* for example, or suggest concentrating on one subject, *Dreams, Sexuality,* or *Self Image through Video*, to quote just a few.

---

[96] The word *groupe* comes from the Italian vocabulary of the 16th century: *gruppo* which designates a single sculpture that includes several people.

[97] Or both together (parental image) in the big group.

• Ongoing groups

These are weekly evening sessions or monthly weekend sessions, for example, and allow a deeper therapeutic work. They are either "closed," that is, all participants enter and leave the group at the same time, after a number of sessions decided in advance, or "slow-open" groups, that is, a new person only comes into the group when another leaves. A minimal engagement, for example of four consecutive sessions, assures the stability of the group. This second formula allows the group to be "the carrier of a long-term story" which accelerates the evolution of new clients.[98] Of these three choices, the ongoing group, followed for one or several years, is the only one that allows for truly deep psychotherapeutic work.

> *John's arrival in the ongoing group (one weekend a month) is difficult: he is disorientated by having to "share his therapist," is aggressive with the others, probably from a fear of rejection. I make the mistake of being too quick to want to help him to elucidate what is happening in our relationship. The therapeutic alliance no longer exists.*
>
> *Once again, I describe the development of my work with him in my supervision session, to better understand why I now feel so irritated by him. My reaction to his transference is clear: I had represented "his mother" for two years, and I've had enough. I would like him to also see me as a symbolic father or as the man that I am.*
>
> *Since I have a plan for him, this takes me out of the "I-Thou relationship" and puts an "I-It relationship" in its place: "I know what your problem is and what is good for you." And of course, John resists this energetically.*
>
> *I feel relieved to have clarified the "how" of the relationship and I wait for the next opportunity to work on this theme. In the following session,*

---

[98] Masquelier G., « L'appartenance tribale dans les groupes thérapeutiques "lentement" ouverts, » in *Revue Gestalt,* number 13-14, May 1998, pages 131-144.

> *a participant is working on a dream in which I appear. Suddenly John takes the floor and speaks of me in the feminine: "Gonzague, she said..." I smile, he realizes his slip. It's the ideal occasion to put into words what we are feeling; all the members of the group also express their feelings towards John. The group situation has brought something to light: he at last realizes that he was tying me up in knots and that I let myself be tied up, in the sort of relationship that he hates!*
>
> *So, I abandon my plan for him, he abandons his projections onto me, and the therapy continues for another two years.*

I helped him to become aware of how he repeats (with me and the members of the group) a past and painful situation: how he manages to get himself rejected as his mother rejected him.

This example shows just how much Gestalt is a therapy of process: when the relationship is stuck, the creative adjustment disappears and the therapist may question what he is doing with this client, during his supervision session.

To expose one's difficulties in front of a group is sometimes a difficult experience but it is often a catalyst for change. In a Gestalt group, the participants encourage one another to let their defenses down, since they may be an obstacle to a greater authenticity. This accelerates the therapeutic process. The social life in the group highlights the gap between what the clients say of themselves and what they are living.

> *So John affirms in words that he has no problem with women. But the women's feedback—about his systematic avoidance of them during breaks for example—are an eye-opener for him. He then replaces the "I have no problem" with "I have no contact" and allows the suffering that this avoidance generates to emerge.*

John was therefore confronted *in vivo* with what really happens in his relationship with women, when he himself had a different picture of it. The group allows him to readjust his personality-function, that is, to modify the perception that he has of himself: I share with John, and with many others, the feeling that group therapy is the most pertinent therapeutic innovation of the last fifty years.

Some professionals see a difference between:
• Gestalt **within** a group, where each individual pursues his own progress in front of the group which is used as an experimental field, for feedback and as an emotional support. That is the formula that I habitually use.
• **Group** Gestalt,[99] in which personal development is obtained as a result of the group's development. The therapist then sees the group as a whole as being his client. In a therapy group, three elements interact dynamically: *intra-psychic* (for each member), *interpersonal* (between individuals) and *group* (in considering the group as an organism). Those who develop a practice **within** a group, concentrate principally on the first two dynamics, those who have a **group** practice, on the last two dynamics. Perls and Goodman both practiced group Gestalt quite a bit, but described the self at the contact-boundary of a lone organism with its environment. Can one, at least as a metaphor, talk about the *group self*?

A necessary eclecticism

John's case, classic in its content, that is, a difficult contact with his mother in childhood which later disturbs his relationship with adults, can serve to illustrate various therapeutic strategies:
• a Psychoanalyst would allow the transference to happen as a repetition of his childhood situation, which would incite him to "go back into the past" through memories, dreams, slips, etc;

---

[99] A formula developed notably in Cleveland (US) and by Jean Van Pevenage in Brussels and Paris.

• a Rogerian therapist would develop empathetic listening and an unconditional acceptance of John's suffering so that he might free himself from his emotional blockages;

• as a Gestalt therapist, I concentrate on current communication problems. Taking a sympathetic approach, I rely on my own life, present and past, to try to highlight all the difficulties of communication. Group work highlights the repetition of these disturbances with different partners.

But all the methodological studies show that therapists are less and less likely to use only one approach and more likely to integrate different viewpoints in their work. The majority of professionals have had several different types of training. The therapist's personality and that of the client, along with the quality of the therapeutic alliance, are therefore more important than techniques or labels. Dogmatic quarrels between the different approaches are fading in favor of a necessary clinical eclecticism. Group therapy is amplifying this phenomenon.

If the content of sessions then has a tendency to be more similar regardless of the differing schools of thought, it is in specifying the theoretical and explanatory models that practitioners diverge. An example: in therapy with a child, almost all practitioners use play, drawing, storytelling etc, because words are not enough. But differences appear with regard to interpretation, the theory of the psycho-emotional development of the child, etc., that is, what the professionals say or write about their approach.

The professional ethics of the Gestalt therapist

As soon as one addresses the field of psychotherapy, the question of professional ethics arises. Indeed, the transference phenomena are often very intense and the therapist must work within a very clear framework, in order to avoid various problem areas (psychological pressures, financial or sexual exploitation, etc.).

The Gestalt therapist, in looking to establish an I-Thou relationship, that is, an important personal involvement, must be particularly clear on this subject.

Indeed, all professional organizations require their certified members to sign a code of professional ethics[100] and to have in place a system of personal supervision.

At least four themes must be made clear at the start of therapy and are required within the therapeutic framework:

• **The confidentiality rule** involves the therapist in the exercise of his profession, but equally applies to all group participants.

• **Sexual abstinence** guarantees that a client can bring up the whole of his emotional or sexual desires, without ambiguity.

• **No acting out**—especially as regards violence. An emotional sequence, for example on the theme of anger, implies that everyone has integrated this rule, guaranteeing everyone's physical safety.

• **Clarity as regards money**. It's important that the contract should be clear in this area. If a voluntarily missed session needs to be paid for, what happens in the case of an unforeseen problem (transport strike, illness, etc.)?

---

[100] See in the appendix the professional code of ethics of the EAP (European Association of Pyschotherapy).

Other areas where Gestalt can be applied

CHAPTER 8

I n the previous chapters, I evoked only the therapeutic possibilities. Professionals skilled in Gestalt techniques who use this approach in their work as trainers, social workers or psychiatric nurses, for example, are certainly as numerous as *stricto sensu* therapists but they make up a group with possibly ill-defined boundaries.

There are those who emphasize the Gestalt aspect, like the consultant who suggests to managing directors "With Gestalt, you can mobilize your human resources!" Others use Gestalt techniques with, for example, drug addicts, prisoners, hospital patients, yoga teachers in training or students.

Another group is made up of people who prefer to "travel incognito." Without changing their job description, for example, teaching the unemployed how to find a job, they have an efficient tool to make their work more dynamic: their course encourages students to "do Gestalt" without realizing it!

In these cases, Gestalt, having lost its label of "psychotherapy," is becoming an art form, a pedagogical method, a descriptive model of what happens during contact, or a tool which helps communication.[101] Let's look at three important areas where the Gestalt approach is used, that is, training, consulting and coaching.

---

[101] Masquelier G., "La Gestalt" in *Guide des méthodes et pratiques en formation,* under the direction of E. Marc and J. Garcia-Locqueneux, Paris, Retz, 1995, pages 146-157.

Training

Most training sessions take place intra, that is, within a company. This is quite appropriate, since the Gestalt trainer wants to come as close as possible to the everyday reality of the participants and each course is "recreated anew" to adapt to the specific needs that have been determined. There are several fundamental differences between therapy and training, and any confusion between the two can lead to serious consequences.

• Therapy is a dual relationship (even within the context of a group), while training is **triangular**: the need is formulated by a third person, who is generally the person paying for training.

• The object of training is clear, formulated as **objectives**. Generally it is the person who pays for training who fixes the objectives. It usually involves helping the participants to develop a particular ability, or to resolve a difficulty. There is therefore a contract which is also tripartite.

• The **confidentiality** rule is difficult to observe. Training is limited in time. The course members are going to return to their daily lives in the firm and see one another professionally, probably in hierarchical relationships. The training organizer will, justifiably, want an evaluation of the course. It is wise to clarify from the beginning what needs to stay in the group (for example everything that is personal) and what can be said outside the group. Therefore, rather than being secretive, the trainer must be discreet.[102]

---

[102] For example, he can agree to give information on the life of the group, but not on individuals.

A training example

I have chosen this example because I invested quite a bit of time and energy on it myself, and it seems to me to be typical of what a Gestalt approach can bring to a company. The RATP, which manages the Parisian metro system, became aware that each year the number of travelers was diminishing. An in-depth sociological report showed that the category of travelers who were travelling the least were unaccompanied women: especially those who had to travel after eight o'clock in the evening. A strong feeling of danger was emphasized by them during non-directive interviews.

The statements effectively said: "It feels like there aren't any RATP representatives in the corridors, a metro station feels like an empty house, or worse, they are inhabited by street people." In fact, each metro line is autonomous, with a "stationary" staff of around four hundred people ("stationary" meaning that the drivers, repair men, etc., are not included).

"If the public feels it doesn't ever see anyone around, it's partly because the station staff are not sufficiently presenting themselves," one of the interview team stated.

Two decisions were then made by the Management:
• the re-establishment of uniforms, or at least a distinctive sign (special tie, scarf or insignia in the firm's colors) so that the staff could be easily identified by the public;
• the promotion of "a new station service" in which staff would be encouraged to leave the "goldfish bowl" (where tickets are on sale) to be more present in the corridors and available to travelers. There was immediate resistance to this by staff and a training course was planned. This was in 1993.

Several training organizations were invited to bid for the contract. All our rivals suggested very technical approaches, for example, how to welcome passengers, different types of travelers, how to deal with aggressiveness, etc., in short, a "tools" training. On the contrary, we developed the idea that there is no point in giving "helpful hints" if each employee is not given the time to express his fears about meeting travelers while unprotected, the relative security they feel by staying "in the goldfish bowl," etc. We reiterated that the need for communication cannot be imposed from above or made a rule, but that it develops naturally once conditions are suitable.[103]

Gestalt, presented as "the art of making contact", seemed to be right for this situation. We wanted to replace "putting out a message" with "getting in touch with. "

> *In agreement with the different partners: management, trainers, staff and unions, we put together a three-part course:*
>
> *The first part lasting **three days**—at least one day for confidence building and the identification of different barriers to communication, then role-plays based on two or three professional situations (how the first contact with others and the environment can take place while respecting each person's individual needs), and the identification of possible difficulties.*
>
> *Next, an inter-session period lasting about **a month** with a double objective: identifying in the field the obstacles or progress in that area, so as to bring concrete cases to the second session; getting together with their immediate bosses for a meeting on this theme; and then, suggesting possible improvements.*

---

[103] In Gestalt jargon, we'd say, "there is no longer any creative adjustment in the contact between travelers and staff."

*Finally, a second meeting lasting **two days**, designed to deal with the points brought up in the inter-session, and to improve relationship-building abilities.[104]*

During three years, we trained more than six hundred people, on three different metro lines. Each time we started by training management and supervising teams, so that staff could feel strong support from the hierarchy.

The first courses were the most difficult, because our approach was in great contrast to usual training methods in this company.

Then, word-of-mouth gave us a positive image and the new course members were more and more motivated. Several projects, planned during the inter-session and designed to improve contact with the public, began to emerge.

We then organized Gestalt training for four in-house trainers, so they could continue the work on other lines. By alternating didactic courses, co-animation in the field, and meetings with course members from other companies, we showed them our main techniques; finally, we maintained a supervision for these trainers.

This long-term work profoundly changed the quality of human relationships on these three metro lines. We are now continuing this work in several urban transport companies which are dealing with violence in difficult suburbs. In one of the companies, our proposals were chosen with the following comment by the personnel director: "I'm choosing your organization, because you are therapists; so you know the limits of involvement in a company and won't do "unofficial" therapy!" To me, that was a great compliment.

The work of consulting

Whereas the trainer organizes courses, the consultant has more the role of auditor, that is, assessment, and then suggests a plan of action. The consultant gives a new viewpoint to the company or the institution.

Analysis work can be accomplished through observation, interviews, or questionnaires. It is striking to note that some organizations tend to be dysfunctional around the very symptoms they are supposed to be treating. For example: many hospitals suffer from a lack of communication, although work on the psychosomatic aspects of illness has shown the importance of the quality of relationships in a treatment. So any intervention which can facilitate fluidity of communication among hospital staff or with patients, increases the efficiency of the medical treatment.

The difficulty lies in allowing an institution, or more often its management team, to put itself once more into a process of change, of creative adjustment, without losing face. Often the unconscious request of the team is, "Consultant-mirror on the wall, tell me I am the fairest of them all."

It is also important to take the time to establish a solid "I-Thou relationship" with the whole of the team, which then makes it possible to look at the "It" of the symptom, that is, to tackle the institutional dysfunction...

> *I was involved with a team of educators working with delinquents in a working class area of Paris. It took me a long time to find a way of communicating to them what I had seen as evident from our first contact. This team had recreated within itself conflicts around the "law" and the limits imposed, and felt rebellious towards the hierarchy... But how can an educator address his own delinquency, his own rejection of the law?*

Three tools helped me:

• **Paradox work** around polarities: how to be "the worst professional imaginable," by accepting one's own delinquent tendencies?

• **Role play**—to test what a marginal person who is taken in hand by "a representative of society" might feel towards the person to whom he attributes a repressive role;

• **The highlighting of the double contact-boundary**: team-delinquents and team-council. As long as the demands of these two contact-boundaries had nothing in common, the team would only keep blowing out, like a fuse.

The work of the consultant is therefore often concentrated on the contact cycle and resistances. What happens between the company and its clients, between the different departments, between the different hierarchical levels? Here we are referring to a socio-Gestalt, that is, the study of interactions between an organization and its environment. The client is the institution, considered as an organism, in a given field.

Coaching

This term has been fashionable for several years. It comes from the word "coach" in the sporting world. The idea that a world-class athlete should need a coach both for his physical and mental training has become acceptable in the world of business. The life of a manager can be compared to that of an athlete: he needs to establish a plan of action, cope with stress, communicate all the time, etc.

The term "coaching" is therefore used in working with an individual or a small group. The Gestalt coach is a specialist in communication: he helps his client gain some perspective and look at the hidden side of a difficulty, to define his real needs and to recognize his limitations.

Sessions usually take place in half-days, on demand or at set times.[105] The private life of the client only comes up in relation to his professional life. The coach doesn't give advice, in accordance with the Gestalt approach, and doesn't interpret, but suggests experiments so that the client can find his own solution.

For example, let us take a look at a work tool constructed by Serge Ginger,[106] the "pentagram": a star with five branches is the traditional symbol for man, with a head, two arms and two legs.

These five branches represent for him, in this order:
- the physical dimension: the body, motor functions, vitality;
- the emotional dimension: the heart, feelings;
- the rational dimension: the head, ideas, the imagination, creativity;
- the social dimension: relationships with others, cultural life;

---

[105] Every six weeks, for example.
[106] Ginger S., in *Former à l'hôpital,* Toulouse, Privat, 1983, pages 279-304.

- the spiritual dimension: man in his environment, the search for meaning, ethics.

Each individual develops these branches to a greater or lesser extent; our western world sometimes values "head" qualities to the detriment of "heart" qualities. Through experimenting or amplification, we look to re-establish a balance for these different facets.

These five branches can be used as a guideline in the global exploration of a professional environment. I suggest a series of seven sessions, first, the initial contact, then five other sessions for each branch of the star and a final summing-up session. This framework allows for a well-structured approach which works on a deep level, adapted to managerial language.

Often, "unfinished business" experienced by a managing director can lead to a series of failures, of abandonment, of "wounds" received or given, and highlighting them can allow the "boil" to be lanced.

When transposed into a diagram for a manager or a small group, the pentagram can be drawn like this:

My commitment

In my opinion, the beneficial effects of Gestalt Therapy need to go beyond the restricted framework of traditional treatment. All psychotherapeutic approaches have a social role to play, through their ability to give meaning to psychological phenomena, inside everyone and between groups. It is not by chance that all dictatorships begin by muzzling the press and forbidding psychotherapy.[107] Waiting for the explicit need of a client can be a

---

[107] The fall of the Berlin Wall, for example, allowed the development of psychotherapy in Eastern Europe: Gestalt therapy has rapidly developed there.

trap because information is still lacking in this domain. Many people have no idea what personal development could bring them and think that therapy is "just for crazy people! "

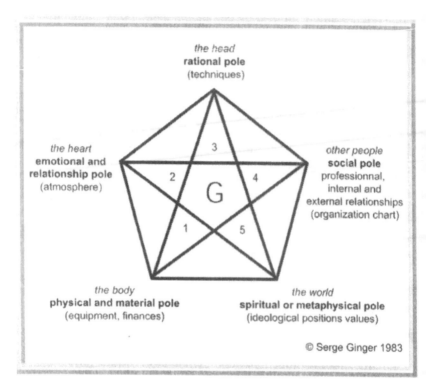

the head
rational pole
(techniques)

the heart
**emotional and
relationship pole**
(atmosphere)

other people
social pole
professionnal,
internal and
external relationships
(organization chart)

3

2   **G**   4

1   5

the body
physical and material pole
(equipment, finances)

the world
spiritual or metaphysical pole
(ideological positions values)

© Serge Ginger 1983

As for Gestalt Therapy, it is to me one of the best adapted psychotherapeutic approaches for social work. Indeed, by not installing transference as the principal motor of treatment, in placing the re-establishment of the contact capacities as the axis of the work, the Gestalt practitioner can be a vector for change in our permanently changing world.

The situation in France

The pioneer years

W e have already seen, in the historical section of this book, that Gestalt courses were available[108] in France from 1971 onwards, and that the first structured training courses started in 1979 with teachers from Quebec. This period saw the development and beginnings of the organization of Gestalt professionals in France: Marie Petit published the first French book entitled *Gestalt, Therapy of the Here and Now*,[109] in 1980. The German word *Gestalt*, although difficult to pronounce in French, gradually took its place in psycho-sociological vocabulary.

After ten years of organizing Gestalt workshops within the IFEPP, Anne and Serge Ginger opened l'EPG (*Ecole Parisienne de Gestalt*—Parisian Gestalt School) in 1981.[110]

Other training institutes were opened in the provinces at the same time, especially in Bordeaux under Jean-Marie Robine, in Grenoble under Jean-Marie Delacroix, and then Nantes with Jacques Blaize.[111]

---

[108] Especially in the IFEPP (Institut de Formation et d'Etudes Psychosociologiques et Pedagogiques).

[109] Petit M., *La Gestalt, thérapie de l'ici et maintenant*, Paris, First edition. Retz, 1980; third edition, ESF, 1986.

[110] I had the pleasure of being in the first year of students.

[111] The Bordeaux and Grenoble institutes merged in 1987, under the name *Institut francais de Gestalt-thérapie (IFGT)*.

In 1981, all these professionals got together and formed the *Société Française de Gestalt* (SFG). This national association gave itself the task of developing research, organizing conferences and publishing a quality professional magazine.[112] In 1983, an international conference brought together two hundred and fifty people from nine different countries, then three years later, three hundred people assembled from twelve different countries. As for publications, they have gone from twenty five at the beginning of the SFG to now numbering close to eight hundred.

Emerging from the profound questions of its phenomenological and existential European roots, Gestalt Therapy crossed the Atlantic with Fritz and Laura Perls to be enriched by American pragmatism. The Gestalt approach is now strongly implanted in Europe and in France: numerous Europeans are at the cutting edge of contemporary Gestalt.

Two main movements stand out:
- one wishes to remain faithful to the founding texts of the first edition, especially the theory of the self. These Gestaltists recognize Gestalt Therapy only in its original sense;
- the other movement wants to enlarge the areas of application of this approach and use it equally in institutions or in companies. These Gestaltists are therefore developing the Gestalt approach, presented as an art of contact, a philosophy for life, as well as a therapeutic modality, with its very specific intervention framework. It is in this movement that the *Ecole Parisienne de Gestalt*, of which I am currently the director, is situated.[113]

---

[112] *Revue de la SFG* which in fifteen editions has published more than 2,400 pages to date.

[113] This is what justifies the preceeding chapter on the different fields of application.

On the other hand, a curious tendency has appeared in the last few years: whereas it is fashionable to affirm that Fritz Perls was not a "respectable" founding father, the two movements have grown closer to Paul Goodman, the former for his contribution to the theory of the self, the latter for having introduced Gestalt theory into the social and political fields.

But whatever references each movement gives itself, Gestalt therapists, being cautious about introjections and looking for creative adjustment are not likely to want to remain as mere imitators of the two founding fathers.

After fifteen years of action and research together, the *Société Francaise de Gestalt* split into two distinct currents with the creation of the *Collège de Gestalt-thérapie* in 1995. Reactions to this split were very diverse: some people found it quite difficult to accept the split, others found it allowed greater clarity in everyone's positioning. Those passionate about Gestalt found it an opportunity to take out subscriptions to two publications and to attend two annual conferences. Finally, others were reassured in observing that there are about twenty psychoanalytic societies in France and that puts things into another perspective...

The training of professionals

The profession of psychotherapist is still not officially recognized in France, and this situation sometimes allows charlatans to operate; this situation is in the process of changing as new structures are being put into place, thanks to the energy of certain leaders in the profession. At the moment, the only guarantee offered to the public is that of a long and well thought-out training in one of the schools which has been recognized by the profession. After five years of practice, psychotherapists can also be validated by a professional certificate delivered by certain professional organizations.

Our profession differs from:

- psychiatrists, who treat mental illness. However medical schools do not give any specific psychotherapeutic training with one notable exception;[114]

- psychologists, who receive five years of university training which is essentially theoretical, consisting in research, evaluation (case histories and tests) or accompaniment of teams. They are not specifically trained in psychotherapy.

There therefore exists a "third way" according to the expression suggested by the *European Association of Psychotherapy (EAP)*, which federates about seventy thousand psychotherapists, grouped around the *Declaration de Strasbourg* (1990), stipulating that "psychotherapy is a free and autonomous profession, implying a specific and high-level training, which guarantees the diversity of different methods."

There are several schools for Gestalt training in France. They propose a course of study which is relatively homogenous, with nuances associated with the different theoretical positions I have already mentioned above, or the personalities of the school management.

I am choosing to present the *Ecole Parisienne de Gestalt* since it is the school that I know best and one which has trained about eight hundred professionals since 1981.

The Ecole Parisienne de Gestalt

All candidates must have been in personal psychotherapy for at least two years.[115] For this personal work, the choice of method is left up to each person, we find that the diversity of these origins is very enriching.

---

[114] University diploma (DU) of the medical school in Lyon-1, where the Gestalt option is taught by the *Ecole Parisienne de Gestalt.*

[115] This applies equally to those candidates who are psychiatrists or psychologists.

The first cycle of study is open to anyone. It is made up of three elements:
- a year's participation in at least one ongoing Gestalt Therapy group;
- two or three occasional courses allowing them to meet at least three of the trainers of the second cycle of study;
- a theoretical part which takes about ten days in total.

The objective of this cycle of study is an immersion into group Gestalt and a "trial" period on both sides: the candidates decide if this sort of work suits them before getting involved any deeper, and the training team can evaluate the candidates' abilities from the outset.

After a selection process which is carried out by the whole team of trainers based on criteria of general maturity, ability to listen, and creativity (in addition to other pre-requirements), the students then begin the **second cycle of study** which is essentially didactic.

In general, these candidates already have a diploma in the human sciences and practical experience in a job which has contact with the public (doctor, psychologist, social worker, teacher, etc.).[116]

The program is structured in four directions and lasts two years:
- a real-life series of experiences allowing a didactic analysis after each work sequence;
- a systematic study of the theory, methodology and psycho-pathology;

---

[116] The professional origins of the 900 students who have followed a second cycle of study at the EPG: 27% were doctors and paramedics, 23% were social workes, 18% were psychologists, 17% were adult trainers, 9% were teachers and 14% were other diverse professions (engineers, researchers, artists....).

- technical preparation and practical training concerning the exercise of the profession (search for one's own style, professional ethics, legal and fiscal aspects, etc.);
- the elaboration of a thesis relating to a theoretical, methodological or clinical area.

At the end of this second cycle of study, students receive a certificate of Gestalt practitioner. This authorizes them to practice Gestalt under supervision. The term "practitioner" encompasses the different fields of professional practice, independently of any eventual future specialization.

The **third cycle of study** consists of specialization, either in psychotherapy or in organizations (firms and institutions). It lasts another two years and comprises:
- a deepening of psychopathology, whatever the chosen option;[117]
- regular supervision;
- advanced training courses in the chosen specialty.

The complete training therefore takes a minimum of seven years (including two years of personal therapy, three years for the first two cycles of study and two years of specialization). The pedagogy is in line with the norms required for the delivery of the *European Certificate of Psychotherapy (CEP)*.[118] There isn't yet unanimity in Europe regarding the work of trainers or consultants.

About thirty Gestalt training organizations, based in twenty different countries, meet each year in the context of *FORGE*.[119]

---

[117] As psychopathological problems are as weighty in firms as in the field of psychotherapy!

[118] The CEP is delivered by the *European Association of Psychotherapy* (EAP). Representatives of 34 European countries are signatories.

[119] International federation of the organisations of formation (training) in Gestalt.

Since 1991, teams meet to renew their teaching methods and to transmit new research areas; a system of equivalent qualifications and teacher or student exchanges has been created.

Supervision

I have mentioned this term regularly throughout this book. It may seem surprising to a novice that a psychotherapist might need to be supervised throughout his career. This necessity comes from the counter-transference relationship which the therapist experiences with his client: when a difficulty comes up during therapy, supervision allows "light to be shed on what is being played out in the shadows." Indeed one part of this counter-transference is made up of unconscious resonance. The professional is therefore obliged to permanently call himself into question in relation to his clients, each time he notes a difficulty. The Gestalt therapist, by choosing to work in a relation of dialogue, with important personal involvement, feels this need for supervision particularly strongly.

Supervision can take place in a small group or individually. I prefer the group for those starting out in their career: by sharing difficulties with colleagues, by hearing a large cross section of varied cases and delicate situations, each member of the group refines the quality of his work.

In our approach, there are several types of supervision:

- **Technical supervision**

This is designed principally for beginners. Emphasis is placed on the framework of treatment, on therapeutic strategy, on theoretical indicators. The central question is: "What should I do with this client?"

- ## Psychopathological supervision

The projector is turned on the psychological suffering and what in the treatment awakens this suffering. As we saw in chapter three, Gestalt psychopathology is relational, temporal and contextual. The question becomes: "Who is this client in front of me?"

- ## Counter-transference supervision

The therapist then tries to highlight his projections towards his clients, that is, the personal echoes—often unconscious—awakened in him, and all that is played out in the connection of the I-Thou relationship. The supervisor then uses the same intervention strategies as in therapy, that is to say, for example, metaphor, amplification, monodrama, etc. All this to find an answer to the question: "What are we exchanging at our contact-boundaries?"

In practice, all supervisors use these three aspects depending on circumstances, but each develops his own style; that is why therapists find it helpful to change supervisor every two or three years. A good supervisor is not necessarily someone who is much more competent, otherwise who would organize the supervision of the supervisors and the control of the super-supervisors? ! He can be a peer, chosen for his competence and didactic clarity.

In addition to the search for the quality of the relationship, supervision has another use, which I often call informally "the garbage-can effect." Experience has shown us all that one cannot permanently get near to the psychological suffering of others, without giving oneself the tools for sometimes letting go. At times, it's vital to empty one's heart and body which have been filled to the brim with emotions. Supervision is therefore equally a place of replenishment, a time during which tiredness, the general anxiety generated by a client who is not doing well, impatience with a client who is stuck, all can be expressed: in short, a time when the therapist can look after his own psychological health.

A profession in development

There must be in France today about a thousand Gestalt professionals, working freelance or in association. As an indication, of the nine hundred former students of the thirty-seven graduating classes of the *Ecole Parisienne de Gestalt*, somewhat more than half are individual psychotherapists (mostly in private practice), a third organize groups (personal development or therapy) and a further third use Gestalt methods in institutions or businesses.[120] This movement is expanding greatly at this time, in France as well as throughout western Europe.

Gestalt professionals, French organizations and training institutes meet under the umbrella of the *EAGT (European Association for Gestalt Therapy)*, which itself also organizes conferences and delivers accreditation.

Others prefer to meet under multi-referential umbrella groups for the richness of exchanges between different movements. For example the *Syndicat National des Praticiens en Psychotherapy (SNPPsy)* —the National Union of Psychotherapy Practitioners, and the *Federation Francaise de Psychotherapie (FFdP)*—the French Federation of Psychotherapy.

Gestalt Therapy has also influenced many therapists who have integrated certain concepts or certain experiments, without referring only to this approach. You only need to look at the ads of any psychological magazine, to realize that the word *Gestalt* is one of the most frequently used by therapists introducing their approach.

How can we associate these different approaches without losing our identity? In Gestalt terms I would say: "How can we assimilate, without introjection or confluent mechanisms?"

---

[120] This comes to more than 100% as most professionals belong to two of these categories.

A debate on the vocabulary of psychopathology regularly agitates our professional community:

Should we use psychoanalytical concepts,[121] which have the advantage of being well-known in France and allow us to speak "the same language" as many of our colleagues?

Should we adopt the Diagnostic and Statistical Manual (DSM) of the American Psychiatric Association[122] which allows international exchanges and facilitates statistical research as all problems are numerically coded? The manual describes each diagnosis in great detail, without reference to any particular theory.

Or should we create a psychopathological manual and a theory of the development of the personality specific to Gestalt? That is to say, to address these questions in terms of process and contact function.[123] The debate continues...

An eventful life

Gestalt Therapy has recently celebrated its fifty years of life. It was born in the context of the post-war years, of the baby boom, of economic expansion. It has developed a paradigm of unlimited growth: the organism determines what is good for it within the environment thanks to its faculties of creative adjustment, and the "completing of gestalts" is a source of growth. The objective of therapy can thus be seen to encourage the flow of unfolding cycles and to kick-start "unfinished business. "

The free-thinking philosophy of the post-1968 revolutionary years has amplified this belief: Perls and Goodman, in a Rousseau-

---

[121] Laplanche J. and Pontalis J.-B., *Vocabulaire de la psychanalyse*, Paris, PUF 1967.

[122] DSM IV, translated by Guelfi, Paris, Masson 1996.

[123] This subject is adressed in *Regards gestaltistes sur la psychopathologie*, Paris, Société française de Gestalt 1994.

ist perspective affirm that the world is a good place, and presuppose that any need can be met and that it is a source of growth.[124] Expand or die! Both Perls and Goodman fought against introjections to free the oppressive elements of education.

Psychotherapists today work in a quite different context: economic difficulties and the disappearance of social or parental certainties have changed the givens. Gestalt has followed this change: rather than destroying blockages, it is often a question of helping the client to structure himself, to find his bearings in a world of perpetual change.

"Chewing over introjections" to free oneself of them has been replaced by "developing the creative adjustment" to survive. Gestalt therapists have therefore applied to themselves what they suggest to their clients. The need to change, to evolve, to find responses in the social environment, in short not to stay in an "ivory tower." They are creators in their own lives and can, I hope, recognize themselves in the subtitle of this book: "living creatively today."

Perls was probably thinking of all these possibilities when he said: "Gestalt is too good to be reserved only for those who are ill!"

---

[124] Masquelier C., "*Ecueils - Les risques de dérapage liés à la posture ou à la théorie gestaltiste*" in *revue Gestalt,* number 15, december 1998, pages 10-29.

GONZAGUE MASQUELIER
5 rue du Pressoir Coquet
60000 BEAUVAIS
FRANCE

tel: + 33 3 44 45 27 27
fax + 33 3 44 45 27 44

gonzague.masquelier@wanad oo.fr
www.gestalt.asso.fr

Personal bibliography

- MASQUELIER Gonzague, *Drogue ou liberté : un lieu pour choisir.* Paris, éditions universitaires, 1983, 115 p.

- MASQUELIER Gonzague, Gestalt et Pédagogie, in *Les carnets du Yoga,* n° 79, mai 1986, pp. 8-15.

- MASQUELIER Gonzague, La Gestalt en évolution, in *L'impact de la Gestalt dans la société d'aujourd'hui.* Paris, SFG, 1988, pp. 289-294.

- MASQUELIER Gonzague, La Gestalt en France, in revue *Gestalt,* n° 1, SFG, automne 1990, pp. 145-152.

- MASQUELIER Gonzague et BLAIZE Jacques, La Gestalt-thérapie : théorie et méthode, in *Journal des Psychologues,* n° 94, février 1992, pp. 48-52.

- MASQUELIER Gonzague, La Gestalt, in *Guide des méthodes et pratiques en formation,* sous la direction de E. Marc et J. Garcia-Lorqueneux. Paris, Retz, 1995, pp. 146-157.

- MASQUELIER Gonzague, L'appartenance tribale dans les groupes thérapeutiques "lentement" ouverts, in revue *Gestalt,* n° 13-14, SFG, mai 1998, pp. 131-144.

- MASQUELIER Gonzague, *Vouloir sa vie : la Gestalt-thérapie aujourd'hui.* Paris, Retz, 1999, 144 p.

- MASQUELIER Gonzague, analyse de l'Encyclopédie des religions, in revue *Gestalt,* n°17, S.F.G., décembre 1999, pp. 177-179.

- MASQUELIER Chantal et Gonzague, Gestalt overseas, in revue *Gestalt,* n°17, S.F.G., décembre 1999, pp. 161-164.

- MASQUELIER Gonzague, Gestalt et Pédagogie, in *L'insertion par l'ailleurs,* sous la direction de Denis Dubouchet. Paris, La documentation française, 2002, pp. 8-15.

- MASQUELIER Gonzague, Qu'est-ce que la Gestalt-thérapie ?, in *Annuaire 2002 des psychothérapeutes.* Lyon, éditions REEL, 2002, pp. 23-30.

EUROPEAN ASSOCIATION
OF PSYCHOTHERAPY (EAP)

STATEMENT OF ETHICAL PRINCIPLES:

PREAMBLE:

Psychotherapists respect the dignity and worth of the individual and strive for the preservation and protection of fundamental human rights.

They are committed to increasing knowledge of human behaviour and of people's understanding of themselves and others and the utilisation of such knowledge for the promotion of human welfare.

While pursuing these objectives they make every effort to protect the welfare of those who seek their services, of people related to those using their services (where that does not conflict with the needs of their clients) and of any research participants that may be the object of study.

Psychotherapists respect other members of their profession and of related professions and make every effort, in so far as they are able and where that does not conflict with the interests of their clients, to provide full information and give mutual respect.

They use their skills only for purposes consistent with these values and do not knowingly permit their misuse by others.

While demanding for themselves freedom of inquiry and communication, psychotherapists accept the responsibility this freedom requires: competence, objectivity in the application of skills, and concern for the best interests of clients, colleagues, students, research participants, & society members.

In the pursuit of these ideals, psychotherapists subscribe to detailed ethical principles in the following areas, which follow:

1. Responsibility;
2. Competence;
3. Moral & Legal Standards;
4. Confidentiality;
5. Welfare of the Consumer;
6. Professional Relationships;
7. Public Statements;
8. Assessment Techniques;
9. Research.

Psychotherapists cooperate fully with their own professional, national, and European organisations & associations and with the European Association for Psychotherapy (EAP) by responding promptly and completely to inquiries from and requirements of any duly constituted ethics or professional committees of such associations or organisations of which they are a member or to which they belong.

Acceptance onto the Register of the European Certificate for Psychotherapy (ECP) commits a psychotherapist to adherence to all of these principles.

PRINCIPLE 1: RESPONSIBILITY

General Principle: In providing services, psychotherapists maintain the highest standards of their profession. They accept the responsibility for the consequences of their acts and make every effort to ensure that their services are used appropriately.

Principle 1.a: As practitioners, psychotherapists know that they bear a heavy social responsibility because their recommendations and professional actions may alter the lives of others. They are alert to personal, social, organisational, financial, environmental, or political situations and pressures that might lead to misuse of their influence.

Principle 1.b: Psychotherapists clarify in advance with their clients all matters that might pertain to their working together. They avoid relationships that may limit their objectivity or create a conflict of interest.

Principle 1.c: Psychotherapists have the responsibility to attempt to prevent distortion, misuse, or suppression of their findings by an institution or agency of which they are employees.

Principle 1.d: As members of national or organisational bodies, psychotherapists remain accountable as individuals to the highest standards of their profession.

Principle 1.e: As teachers or trainers, psychotherapists recognise their primary obligation to help others acquire knowledge and skill. They maintain high standards of scholarship by presenting information objectively, fully, and accurately.

Principle 1.f: As researchers, psychotherapists accept responsibility for the selection of their research topics and methods used in investigation, analysis and reporting. They plan their research in ways to minimise the possibility that their findings will be misleading. They provide thorough discussion of the limitations of their data, especially where their work touches on social policy or might be construed to the detriment of persons in specific age, sex, ethnic, socio-economic, or other social groups. In publishing reports of their work, they never suppress disconfirming data, and they acknowledge the existence of alternative hypotheses and explanations of their findings. Psychotherapists take credit only for the work they have actually done. They clarify in advance with all appropriate persons and agencies the expectations for sharing and utilising research data. Interference with the

milieu in which data are collected is kept to a minimum.

PRINCIPLE 2: COMPETENCE

General Principle: The maintenance of high standards of competence is a responsibility shared by all psychotherapists in the interest of the public and the profession as a whole. Psychotherapists recognise the boundaries of their competence and the limitations of their techniques. They only provide services and only use techniques for which they are qualified by training and experience. In those areas in which recognised standards do not yet exist, psychotherapists take whatever precautions are necessary to protect the welfare of their clients. They maintain knowledge of current health, scientific and professional information related to the services they render.

Principle 2.a: Psychotherapists accurately represent their competence, education, training, and experience. They claim as evidence of educational & professional training qualifications only those degrees or qualifications obtained from reputable educational institutions or those recognised by the EAP. They ensure that they adequately meet the minimum professional standards as laid down by the EAP, the relevant National Awarding Organisation's criteria, and the criteria of the relevant European Wide Accrediting Organisation in their modality or method, where these exist. They respect the other sources of education, training and experience that they have received.

Principle 2.b: As practitioners, and as teachers or trainers, psychotherapists perform their duties on the basis of careful preparation and readiness so that

160 GESTALT THERAPY : Living Creatively Today

their practice is of the highest standard and communication is accurate, current, and relevant.

Principle 2.c: Psychotherapists recognise the need for continuing education and personal development and are open to new procedures and changes in expectations and values over time.

Principle 2.d: Psychotherapists recognise differences among people, such as those that may be associated with age, sex, socio-economic, and ethnic backgrounds or the special needs of those who might have been specifically disadvantaged. They obtain suitable training, experience, or counsel to assure competent and appropriate service when relating to all such persons.

Principle 2.e: Psychotherapists responsible for decisions involving individuals or policies based on test results have an understanding of psychological or educational measurement, validation problems, and test research.

Principle 2.f: Psychotherapists recognise that personal problems and conflicts may interfere with professional effectiveness. Accordingly they refrain from undertaking any activity in which their personal problems are likely to lead to inadequate performance or harm to a client, colleague, student, or research participant. If engaged in such activity when they become aware of their personal problems, they seek competent professional assistance to determine whether they should suspend, terminate, or limit the scope of their professional activities.

Principle 2.g: Psychotherapists entering into new fields of activity ensure that they have completed all the training and professional requirements related to that field of activity, prior to

practising, and that their activity in this new field is of the highest possible standard. They ensure that there is no dilution of, confusion or conflict with any current activity.

PRINCIPLE 3: MORAL & LEGAL STANDARDS

General Principle:
Psychotherapists' moral and ethical standards of behaviour are a personal matter to the same degree as they are for any other citizen, except where these may compromise the fulfilment of their professional responsibilities or reduce the public trust in psychotherapy & psychotherapists. Regarding their own personal behaviour, psychotherapists are sensitive to prevailing community standards and to the possible impact that conformity to or deviation from these standards may have upon the quality of their performance as psychotherapists. Psychotherapists are also aware of the possible impact of their public behaviour upon the ability of colleagues to perform their professional duties.

Principle 3.a: As professionals, psychotherapists act in accord with the principles of EAP and their National Awarding Organisation's (NAO) and their institute or association's standards and guidelines related to practice. Psychotherapists also adhere to relevant governmental laws and regulations. When European, national, provincial, organisational, or institutional laws, regulations, or practices are in conflict with EAP, the NAO, or their institution or association's standards and guidelines, psychotherapists make known their commitment to EAP, their NAO & their institute or association's standards and guidelines and, wherever possible, work toward a resolution of the conflict. As professionals, they are concerned with the development of such legal and quasi-legal regulations that best serve the public interest, and they work toward changing existing regulations that are not beneficial to the public interest.

Principle 3.b: As employees or employers, psychotherapists do not engage in or condone any practices that are inhumane or that result in illegal or unjustifiable actions. Such practices include, but are not limited to, those based on considerations of race, handicap, age, gender, sexual preference, religion, or national origin in practice, in hiring, promotion, or training.

Principle 3.c: In their professional roles, psychotherapists avoid any action that will violate or diminish the human, legal and civil rights of clients or others who may be affected.

Principle 3.d: As practitioners, teachers, trainers and researchers, psycho-therapists are aware of the fact that their personal values may affect their communication, the use of techniques, selection and presentation of views or materials and the nature or implementation of research. When dealing with topics that may give offence, they recognise and respect the diverse attitudes and individual sensitivities that clients, students, trainees or subjects may have towards such matters.

PRINCIPLE 4: CONFIDENTIALITY

General Principle:

Psychotherapists have a primary obligation to respect the confidentiality of information obtained from persons in the course of their work as psychotherapists. They reveal such infor-mation to others only with the consent of the person (or the person's legal representative), except in those unusual circumstances in which not to do so would probably result in clear danger to the person or to others. Psychotherapists inform their clients of the legal limits of confidentiality. Consent to reveal information to others would normally be obtained in writing from the person concerned.

Principle 4.a: Information obtained in clinical or consulting relationships, or evaluating data concerning children, students, employees, and others, is discussed only for professional purposes and only with persons clearly concerned with the case. Written and oral reports present only data germane to the purposes of the evaluation or for a referral, and every effort is made to avoid undue invasion of privacy.

Principle 4.b: Psychotherapists who present personal information obtained during the course of professional work in writings, lectures, or other public forums either obtain adequate prior consent to do so or adequately disguise all identifying information.

Principle 4.c: Psychotherapists make provisions for maintaining confidentiality in the storage and disposal of records, and in the event of their own unavailability.

Principle 4.d: When working with minors or other persons who are unable to give voluntary, informed consent, psychotherapists take special care to protect these person's best interests and consult others involved appropriately.

PRINCIPLE 5: WELFARE OF THE CLIENT

General Principle:

Psychotherapists respect the integrity and protect the welfare of the people and groups with whom they work. When conflicts of interest arise between clients and psychotherapists' employing institutions, psychotherapists clarify the nature and direction of their loyalties and responsibilities and keep all parties informed of their commitments. Psychotherapists fully inform clients as to the purpose and nature of any evaluative, treatment, educational, or training procedure, and they openly acknowledge that clients, students, trainees, or participants in research have freedom of choice with regard to participation. Coercion of people to participate or to remain in receipt of services is unethical.

Principle 5.a: Psychotherapists are continually cognizant of their own needs and of their potentially influential position vis-à-vis persons such as clients, students, trainees, subjects and subordinates. They avoid exploiting the trust and dependency of such persons. Psychotherapists make every effort to avoid dual relationships that could impair their professional judgment or increase the risk of exploitation. Examples of such dual relationships include, but are not limited to, professional treatment of or research with employees, students, supervisees, close friends, or relatives. Sexual intimacies with any such clients, students, trainees and research participants are unethical.

Principle 5.b: When a psychotherapist agrees to provide services to a client at the request of a third party, the psychotherapist assumes the responsibility of clarifying the nature of the relationships to all parties concerned.

Principle 5.c: Where the demands of an organisation require psychotherapists to violate these or any ethical principles, psychotherapists clarify the nature of the conflict between the demands and the principles. They inform all parties of their ethical responsibilities as psychotherapists and take appropriate action.

Principle 5.d: Psychotherapists make advance financial arrangements that safeguard the best interests of and are clearly understood by their clients, students, trainees or research participants. They neither give or receive and remuneration for referring clients for professional services. They contribute a portion of their services to work for which they receive little or no financial return.

Principle 5.e: Psychotherapists terminate a clinical or consulting relationship as soon as it is reasonably clear that the client is not benefiting from it, or whenever the client requires. They offer to help the client locate alternative sources of assistance.

PRINCIPLE 6: PROFESSIONAL RELATIONSHIPS

General Principle:

Psychotherapists act with due regard for the needs, special competencies, and obligations of their colleagues in psychotherapy, psychology, medicine & other professions. They respect the prerogatives and obligations of the institutions or organisations with which these other colleagues are associated.

Principle 6.a: Psychotherapists understand the areas of competence of related professions. They make full use of all the professional, technical, and administrative resources that serve the best interests of consumers. The absence of formal relationships with other professional workers does not relieve psychotherapists of the responsibility for securing for their clients the best possible professional service, nor does it relieve them of the obligation to exercise foresight, diligence, and tact in obtaining the complementary or alternative assistance needed.

Principle 6.b: Psychotherapists know and take into account the traditions and practices of other professional groups with whom they work and they cooperate fully with such groups. If a person is receiving similar services from another professional, the psychotherapist carefully considers that professional relationship and proceeds with caution and sensitivity to the therapeutic issues as well as the client's welfare. The psychotherapist discusses these issues with the client so as to minimise the risk of confusion and conflict, and seeks, where possible, to maintain clear and agreed relationships with other involved professionals.

Principle 6.c: Psychotherapists who employ or supervise other professionals or professionals in training accept the obligation to facilitate the further professional development of these individuals and take action to ensure their competence.

They provide appropriate working conditions, timely evaluations, constructive consultation, and experience opportunities.

Principle 6.d: Psychotherapists do not exploit their professional relationships with clients, supervisees, students, employees or research participants sexually or otherwise. Psychotherapists do not condone or engage in sexual harassment. Sexual harassment is defined as deliberate or repeated comments, gestures, or physical contacts of a sexual nature that are unwanted by the recipient.

Principle 6.e: When psychotherapists know of an ethical violation by another psychotherapist, and it seems appropriate, they informally attempt to resolve the issue by bringing the behaviour to the attention of the psychotherapist. If the misconduct is of a minor nature and/or appears to be due to lack of sensitivity, knowledge, or experience, such an informal solution is usually appropriate. Such informal corrective efforts are made with sensitivity to any rights to confidentiality involved. If the violation does not seem amenable to an informal solution, or is of a more serious nature, psychotherapists bring it to the attention of the appropriate institution, association or committee on professional ethics and conduct.

Principle 6.f: Publication credit is assigned to those who have contributed to a publication in proportion to their professional contributions. Major contributions of a professional character made by several persons to a common project are recognised by joint authorship with the individual who made the principle contribution listed first. Minor contributions of a professional character and extensive clerical or similar non-professional assistance may be acknowledged in footnotes or in an introductory statement. Acknowledgement through specific citations is made for unpublished as well as published material that has directly influenced the research or writing. Psychotherapists who compile and edit material of others for publication publish the material in the name of the originating group, if appropriate, with their own name appearing as chairperson or editor. All contributors are acknowledged and named.

Principle 6.g: In conducting research in institutions or organisations, psychotherapists secure appropriate authorisation to conduct such research. They are aware of their obligation to future research workers and ensure that host institutions receive adequate information about the research and proper acknowledgements of their contributions.

PRINCIPLE 7: PUBLIC STATEMENTS

General Principle: Public statements, announcements of services, advertising, and promotional activities of psychotherapists serve the purpose of helping the public make informed judgments and choices. Psychotherapists represent accurately and objectively their professional qualifications, affiliations, and functions, as well as those of the institutions or organisations with which they or the statements may be associated. In public statements providing psychotherapeutical information or professional opinions or providing information about the availability of techniques, products, publications, and services, psychotherapists base their statements on generally acceptable findings and techniques with full recognition of the limits and uncertainties of such evidence.

Principle 7.a: When announcing or advertising professional services, psycho-

therapists may list the following information to describe the provider and services provided: name, highest relevant academic degree or training certificate earned from an accredited institution, date, type, award of the ECP, membership of psychotherapy organisations and professionally relevant or related bodies, address, telephone number, office hours, a brief listing of the type of psychological services offered, an appropriate presentation of fee information, foreign languages spoken, policy with regards to insurance or third party payments and other brief & pertinent information. Additional relevant or important consumer information may be included if not prohibited by other sections of these Ethical Principles.

Principle 7.b: In announcing or advertising the availability of psycho-therapeutic services or publications, psychotherapists do not present their affiliation with any organisation in a manner that falsely implies sponsorship or certification by that organisation. In particular and for example, psychotherapists do not state European, national registration or institutional or associational status in a way to suggest that such status implies specialised professional competence or qualifications. Public statements include, but are not limited to, communication by means of periodical, book, list, directory, internet, television, radio, or motion picture. They do not contain (i) a false, fraudulent, misleading, deceptive, or deceptive, or unfair statement; (ii) a misinterpretation of fact or a statement likely to mislead or deceive because in context it makes only a partial disclose of relevant facts; (iii) a testimonial from a patient regarding the quality of a psychotherapist's services or products; (iv) a statement intended or likely to create false or unjustified expectations of favourable results; (v) a statement implying unusual, unique, or one-of-a-kind abilities; (vi) a statement intended or likely to appeal to a client's fears, anxieties, or emotions concerning the possible results of failure to obtain the offered services; (vii) a statement concerning the comparative desirability of offered services; (viii) a statement of direct solicitation of individual clients.

Principle 7.c: Psychotherapists do not compensate or give anything of value to a representative of the press, radio, television, or other communication medium in anticipation of or in return for professional publicity in a news item. A paid advertisement must be identified as such, unless it is apparent from the context that it is a paid advertisement. If communicated to the public by use of radio or television, an advertisement is pre-recorded and approved for broadcast by the psychotherapist. Copies of advertisements and recordings of broadcasts are retained by the psychotherapist.

Principle 7.d: Announcements or advertisements of "personal growth groups," special-interest group sessions, courses, clinics, trainings and agencies give a clear statement of purpose and a clear description of the experiences or training to be provided. The education, training, and experience of the staff members are appropriately specified and available prior to the commencement of the group, training course or services. A clear statement of fees and any contractual implications is available before participation.

Principle 7.e: Psychotherapists associated with the development or promotion of psychotherapeutic techniques, products, books, or other such offered for commercial sale make reasonable efforts to ensure that announcements and advertisements are presented in a professional, scientifically acceptable, ethical and factually informative manner.

Principle 7.f:Psychotherapists do not participate for personal gain in commercial announcements or advertisements recommending to the public the purchase or use of proprietary or single-source products or services when that participation is based solely upon their identification as psycho-therapists.

Principle 7.g: Psychotherapists present the science and art of psychotherapy and offer their services, products, and publications fairly and accurately, avoiding misrepresentation through sensationalism, exaggeration, or superficiality. Psychotherapists are guided by the primary obligation to aid the public in developing informed judgments, opinions, and choices.

Principle 7.h: As teachers, psycho-therapists ensure that statements in catalogues and course outlines are accurate and not misleading, particularly in terms of subject matter to be covered, bases for evaluating progress, and the nature of course experiences. Announcements, brochures or advertisements describing workshops, seminars, or other educational programs accurately describe the audience for which the program is intended as well as eligibility requirements, educational objectives, and nature of the materials to be covered. These announcements also accurately represent the education, training, and experience of the psychotherapists presenting the programs and any fees involved.

Principle 7.i: Public announcements or advertisements soliciting research participants in which clinical services or other professional services are offered as an inducement make clear the nature of the services as well as the costs and other obligations to be accepted by participants in the research.

Principle 7.j: A psychotherapist accepts the obligation to correct others who represent the psychotherapist's professional qualifications, or associations with products or services, in a manner incompatible with these guidelines.

Principle 7.k: Individual diagnostic and therapeutic services are provided only in the context of a professional psychotherapeutic relationship. When personal advice is given by means of public lectures or demonstrations, newspaper or magazine articles, radio or television programs, mail, or similar media, the psychotherapist utilises the most current relevant data and exercises the highest level of professional judgment.

Principle 7.l: Products that are described or presented by means of public lectures or demonstrations, newspaper or magazine articles, radio or television programs, mail, or similar media meet the same recognised standards as exist for products used in the context of a professional relationship.

PRINCIPLE 8: ASSESSMENT TECHNIQUES

General Principle: In the development, publication, and utilisation of psychotherapeutic or psychological assessment techniques, psychotherapists make every effort to promote the welfare and best interests of the client. They guard against the misuse of assessment results. They respect the client's right to know the results, the interpretations made, and the bases for their conclusions and recommendations. Psychotherapists make every effort to maintain the security of tests and other assessment techniques within the limits of legal mandates. They strive to ensure the appropriate use of assessment techniques by others.

Principle 8.a: In using assessment techniques, psychotherapists respect the right of clients to have full explanations of the nature and purpose of the techniques in language the clients can understand, unless an explicit exception to this right has been agreed upon in advance. When the explanations are to be provided by others, psychotherapists establish procedures for ensuring the adequacy of these explanations.

Principle 8.b: Psychotherapists responsible for the development and standardisation of psychological tests and other assessment techniques utilise established scientific procedures and observe the relevant EAP, national, and institutional or organisational standards.

Principle 8.c: In reporting assessment results, psychotherapists indicate any reservations that exist regarding the validity or reliability because of the circumstances of the assessment or the inappropriateness of the norms for the person tested.

Psychotherapists strive to ensure that the results of assessments and their interpretations are not misused by others.

Principle 8.d: Psychotherapists recognise that assessment results may become obsolete and do not represent a complete picture of the assessed. They make every effort to avoid and prevent the misuse of obsolete measures or incomplete assessments.

Principle 8.e: Psychotherapists offering scoring and interpretation services are able to produce appropriate evidence for the validity of the programs and procedures used in arriving at interpretations. The public offering of an interpretation service is considered a professional-to-professional consultation. Psychotherapists make every effort to avoid misuse of assessment reports.

Principle 8.f: Psychotherapists do not encourage or promote the use of psychotherapeutic or psychological assessment techniques by inappropriately trained or otherwise unqualified persons through teaching, sponsorship, or supervision.

PRINCIPLE 9: RESEARCH

General Principle: The decision to undertake research rests upon a considered judgment by the individual psychotherapist about how best to contribute to human science and human welfare. Having made the decision to conduct research, the psychotherapist considers alternative directions in which research energies and resources might be invested. On the basis of this consideration, the psychotherapist carries out the investigation with respect and concern for the dignity and welfare of the people who participate and with

cognisance of regulations and professional standards governing the conduct of research with human participants.

Principle 9.a: In planning a study, the psychotherapist who carries out the investigation (the investigator) has the responsibility to make a careful evaluation of its ethical acceptability. To the extent that the weighing of scientific and human values suggests a compromise of any principle, the investigator incurs a correspondingly serious obligation to seek ethical advice and observe stringent safeguards to protect the rights of human participants.

Principle 9.b: Considering whether a participant in a planned study will be a "subject at risk" or a "subject at minimal risk", according to recognised standards, is of primary ethical concern to the investigator.

Principle 9.c: The investigator always retains the responsibility for ensuring ethical practice in research. The investigator is also responsible for the ethical treatment of research participants by collaborators, assistants, students, and employees, all of whom, however, incur similar obligations.

Principle 9.d: Except in minimal-risk research, the investigator establishes a clear and fair agreement with research participants, prior to their participation, that clarifies the obligation and responsibilities of each. The investigator has the obligation to honour all promises and commitments in that agreement. The investigator informs the participants of all aspects of the research that might reasonably be expected to influence willingness to participate and explains all other aspects of the research about which the participants inquire. Failure to make full disclosure prior to obtaining informed consent requires additional safeguards to protect the welfare and the dignity of the research participants. Research with children or with participants who have impairments that would limit understanding and/or communication requires special safeguarding procedures.

Principle 9.e: Methodological requirements of a study may make the use of concealment or deception seem necessary. Before conducting such a study, the investigator has a special responsibility to (i) determine whether the use of such techniques is justified by the study's prospective scientific, educational, or implied value; (ii) determine whether alternative procedures are available that do not use concealment or deception; and (iii) ensure that the participants are provided with sufficient explanation as soon as possible. There exists a presumption not to use such techniques.

Principle 9.f: The investigator respects the individual's freedom to decline to participate in or withdraw from the research at any time. The obligation to protect this freedom requires careful thought and consideration when the investigator is in a position of authority or influence over the participant. Such positions of authority include, but are not limited to, situations in which research participation is required as part of employment or in which the participation is a student, client, or employee of the investigator. The rights of the individual predominate over the needs of the investigator to complete the research.

Principle 9.g: The investigator protects the participant from physical

and mental discomfort, harm, and danger that may arise from research procedures. If risks of such consequences exist, the investigator informs the participant of that fact. Research procedures likely to cause serious or lasting harm to a participant are not used unless the failure to use these procedures might expose the participant to risk of greater harm, or unless the research has great potential benefit and fully informed and voluntary consent is obtained from each participant. The participant should be informed of procedures for contacting the investigator within a reasonable time period following participation should stress, potential harm, or related questions or concerns arise. Consent obtained from the participant does not limit their legal rights or reduce the investigator's legal responsibilities.

Principle 9.h: After the data are collected, the investigator provides the participant with information about the nature of the study and attempts to remove any misconceptions that may have arisen. Where scientific or humane values justify delaying or withholding this information, the investigator incurs a special responsibility to monitor the research and to ensure that there are no damaging consequences for the participant.

Principle 9.i: Where research procedures result in undesirable conesquences for the individual participant, the investigator has the responsibility to detect and remove or correct these consequences, including long-term effects.

Principle 9.j: Information obtained about a research participant during the course of an investigation is confidential unless otherwise agreed upon in advance. When the possibility exists that others may obtain access to such information, this possibility, together with the plans for protecting confidentiality, is explained to the participant as part of the procedure for obtaining informed consent.

European Association for Psychotherapy (EAP)

Vienna, July 2002

INTERNATIONAL LEXICON

Many works have not been translated into French. That is why the *International Federation of Gestalt Training Organizations (FORGE)*, with the encouragement of its president Serge Ginger, have put together an international guide to Gestalt Therapy in eight languages (German, English, Spanish, French, Italian, Dutch, Portuguese and Russian) in 1995. This guide contains a list of eighty-two words or expressions and a glossary of about a hundred words, in the eight languages.

The guide can be obtained from *FORGE*, who have given me permission to reproduce an extract, for which I am most grateful. I have chosen about sixty words in three languages to help with the reading of foreign books and to facilitate participation in international conferences.

FRANÇAIS	ENGLISH	ESPANOL
confluence	confluence	confluencia
contact	contact	contacto
contre-transfert	counter-transferance	contratransferencia
cycle de contact	contact cycle	ciclo de contacto
déflexion	deflection	deflexion
effet Zeigarnik	Zeigarnik effect	efecto Zeigarnik
égotisme	egotism	egotismo
évitement	avoidance	evitacion
expérimentation	experiment	experimrentacion
feed-back ou rétro-action	feedback	feedback

FRANÇAIS	ENGLISH	ESPANOL
figure/fond	figure/ground	figura/fondo
fonctions de contact	contact functions	funcion de contacto
formation	training	fomacion
forme	form	forma
frontière-contact	contact-boundary	frontera-contacto
Gestalt-psychologie	Gestalt psychology	psicologia Gestalt
homéostasie	homeostasis	homeostasis
ici et maintenant	here and now	aqui y ahora
implication contrôlée	controlled involvment	implicacion controlada
inachevé (travail, gestalt)	unfinished (business)	inacabada
inconscient	unconscious	inconsciente
introjection	introjection	introyeccion
je/tu	I/Thou	Yo/Tu
métaphore	metaphor	metafora
micro-geste	micro-movement	microgestos
mise en action	enactment	puesta en accion
mode moyen	middle mode	modo medio
moi	ego	Yo
monodrame	monodrama	monodrama
maintenant et comment	now and how	ahora y como
passage à l'acte	acting out	pasaje al acto
personnalité	personality	personalidad
polarités	polarities	polaridades
post-contact	post-contact	poscontacto
pré-contact	fore-contact	precontacto
processus	process	proceso
projection	projection	proyeccion
psychologie humaniste	humanistic psychology	psicologia humanista
résistances	resistances	resistencias

FRANÇAIS	ENGLISH	ESPANOL
ressenti corporel	body feeling	el sentir corporal
retrait	withdrawal	retirada
rétroflexion	retroflection	retroflexion
rêve	dream	sueno
rêverie-éveillée	fantasy	sueno despierto
self ou soi	self	si mismo
setting ou cadre	setting	setting
situation inachevée	unfinished business	situacion inacabada
socio-Gestalt	Socio-Gestalt	socio-Gestalt
stress	stress	estrés
sympathie	sympathy	simpatia
transfert	transference	transferencia

Gonzague MASQUELIER
5 rue du Pressoir Coquet
60000 BEAUVAIS
FRANCE
tel: + 33 3 44 45 27 27
fax + 33 3 44 45 27 44
gonzague.masquelier@wanadoo.fr
www.gestalt.asso.fr

SELECTED TITLES FROM GESTALTPRESS

Back to the Beanstock: Enchantment and Reality for Couples
Judith R. Brown

The Dreamer and the Dream: Essays and Reflections on Gestalt
Therapy
Rainette Eden Fants, Edited by Arthur Roberts

A Well-Lived Life: Essays in Gestalt Therapy
Sylvia Fleming Crocker

From the Radical Center: The Heart of Gestalt Therapy
Erving & Miriam Polster

Beyond Individualism: Toward a New Understranding of Self,
Relationship and Experience
Gordon Wheeler

Sketches: An Anthology of Essays, Art and Poetry
Joseph C. Zinker

The Heart of Development: Gestalt Approaches to Working with
Children, Adolescents and Their Worlds (2 Volumes)
Mark McConville & Gordon Wheeler, Editors

Body of Awareness: A Somatic and Developmental Approach to
Psychotherapy
Ruella Frank

Values of Connection: A Relational Approach to Ethics
Robert G. Lee, Editor

Windowframes: Learning the Art of Gestalt Play Therapy the Oaklander
Way
Peter Mortola

Reading Paul Goodman
Gordon Wheeler, Editor

Gestalt Therapy: Living Creatively Today
Gonzague Masquelier

The Evolution of Gestalt Therapy
Deborah Ullman & Gordon Wheeler, Editors